Textile

EDITED BY
CATHERINE HARPER
AND DORAN ROSS

THE JOURNAL OF
CLOTH AND CULTURE

VOLUME 5
ISSUE 3
FALL 2007

ORDERING INFORMATION

Three Issues per volume. One volume per annum.
2007: Volume 5

ONLINE
www.bergpublishers.com

BY MAIL
Berg Publishers
C/O Turpin Distribution Services
Pegasus Drive
Stratton Business Park
Biggleswade
Bedfordshire SG18 8TQ
UK

BY FAX
+ 44 (0)1767 601640

BY TELEPHONE
+ 44 (0)1767 604951

For Subscription Enquiries
email custserv@turpin-distribution.com

ENQUIRIES
Editorial: Kathryn Earle, Managing Editor,
email kearle@bergpublishers.com

Production: Ken Bruce,
email kbruce@bergpublishers.com

Advertising: Veruschka Selbach,
email vselbach@bergpublishers.com

SUBSCRIPTION DETAILS
Free Online Subscription for Print Subscribers.

Full color images available online.

Access your electronic subscription through
www.ingentaconnect.com

Institutional base list subscription price:
US$250.00, £140.00

Individuals' subscription price: US$79.00, £46.00

Berg Publishers is the imprint of
Oxford International Publishers Ltd.

EDITORS

Catherine Harper
University of Brighton, UK

Doran Ross
UCLA Fowler Museum of Cultural History

Associate Editor
Mary Littrell, Colorado State University
mlittrel@cah.colostate.edu

Pennina Barnett, Goldsmiths College
p.barnett@gold.ac.uk

Editorial Assistant
Janet Gilburt
rooster.gilburt@virgin.net

Book Reviews Editor:
Victoria Mitchell, Norwich School of Art & Design, St George Street, Norwich NR3 1BB, UK
v.mitchell@nsad.ac.uk

Exhibition Reviews Editors:
UK and Rest of World
Jennifer Harris, The Whitworth Art Gallery, University of Manchester, Whitworth Park, Manchester M15 6ER, UK
jennifer.harris@man.ac.uk

USA
Geraldine Ondrizek, Art Department Chair, Reed College, Portland, OR 97202, USA
ondrizeg@reed.edu

Rebecca Stevens, Contemporary Textiles, The Textile Museum, 23250 S Street NW, Washington, DC 20008-4088, USA
stevensgrj@aol.com

AIMS AND SCOPE

Cloth accesses an astonishingly broad range of human experiences. The raw material from which things are made, it has various associations: sensual, somatic, decorative, functional and ritual. Yet although textiles are part of our everyday lives, their very familiarity and accessibility belie a complex set of histories, and invite a range of speculations about their personal, social and cultural meanings. This ability to move within and reference multiple sites gives textiles their potency.

This journal brings together research in textiles in an innovative and distinctive academic forum for all those who share a multifaceted view of textiles within an expanded feld. Representing a dynamic and wide-ranging set of critical practices, it provides a platform for points of departure between art and craft; gender and identity; cloth, body and architecture; labor and technology; techno-design and practice—all situated within the broader contexts of material and visual culture.

Textile invites submissions informed by technology and visual media, history and cultural theory; anthropology; philosophy; political economy and psychoanalysis. It draws on a range of artistic practices, studio and digital work, manufacture and object production.

Berg Publishers is a member of CrossRef

INTERNATIONAL ADVISORY BOARD

Ingrid Bachmann
Concordia University, Canada

Elizabeth Barber
Occidental College, USA

Dilys Blum
Philadelphia Museum of Art, USA

Grace Cochrane
Powerhouse Museum, Australia

Susan Conway
Parson's School of Design, USA, and the British Museum, UK

Jasleen Dhamija
Independent Scholar/Consultant, India

Ian Hunter
Manchester Metropolitan University, UK

Janis Jefferies
Goldsmiths College, UK

Sarat Maharaj
Goldsmiths College, University of London, UK

Claire Pajaczkowska
Middlesex University, UK

John Picton
School of Oriental and African Studies, University of London, UK

Mary Schoeser
Freelance Historian, USA and UK

Lotus Stack
Minneapolis Institute of the Arts, USA

Nick Stanley
Birmingham Institute of Art and Design, UK

Anne Wilson
The School of the Art Institute of Chicago, USA

Diana Wood Conroy
University of Wollongong, Australia

SUBMISSIONS

Should you have a topic you would like us to consider, please send an abstract of 300–500 words to one of the editors. Notes for Contributors can be found at the back of the journal and style guidelines are available by emailing kbruce@bergpublishers.com or from the Berg website (www.bergpublishers.com).

© 2007 Berg. All rights reserved. No part of this publication may be reproduced or utilized in any form or by any means, electronic or mechanical, including photocopying and recording, or by any information storage or retrieval system, without permission in writing from the publisher.

ISSN: 1475-9756
www.bergpublishers.com

Textile is indexed by Abstracts in Anthropology; AIO (Anthropological Index Online); Art Bibliographies Modern; Design and Applied Arts Index; Arts and Humanities Citation Index; Current Contents/Arts and Humanities; IBR (International Bibliography of Book Reviews of Scholarly Literature and Social Sciences); IBSS (International Bibliography of the Social Sciences); IBZ (International Bibliography of Periodical Literature on Humanities and Social Sciences); World Textiles.

254 Patched, Louse-ridden, Tattered: Clean and Dirty Clothes
Ingun Grimstad Klepp

276 Joseph Conrad's "The Planter of Malata": Timing, and the Forgotten Adventures of the Silk Plant "Arghan"
Ann Lane

300 Returning Navajo-Churro Sheep for Navajo Weaving
Susan M. Strawn and Mary A. Littrell

320 Exhibition Review
"Lines of Sight": Diane Samuels Tapestry of Glass
Reviewed by Dara Meyers-Kingsley

328 Exhibition Review
On Memory: Deborah Aschheim at the Mattress Factory
Reviewed by Lotus Grenier

332 Exhibition Review
Lia Cook: Re-Embodied
Reviewed by Judith Leemann

340 Exhibition Review
Margie Neuhaus: Sensory Jetty
Reviewed by Heidi Leugers

348 Exhibition Review
Radical Lace and Subversive Knitting
Reviewed by Julie Reiss

356 Book Reviews
Art Textiles of the World: Scandinavia
Reviewed by Caroline Broadhead

The Sculpture of Ruth Asawa: Contours in the Air
Reviewed by Lesley Millar

Contents

EDITORS

Catherine Harper
School of Architecture and Design
University of Brighton
Grand Parade
Brighton BN2 4AY
UK
Catherine.Harper@brighton.ac.uk

Doran Ross
UCLA
Fowler Museum of Cultural History
308 Charles Young Drive
Los Angeles, CA 90095-1549
USA
dross@arts.ucla.edu

Reinventing Textiles
Volume 1: Tradition and Innovation

Reinventing Textiles
Volume 2: Gender and Identity

Reinventing Textiles
Volume 3: Postcolonialism and Creativity
Reviewed by Judith Duffey Harding

Findings: The Material Culture of Needlework and Sewing
Reviewed by Barbara Burman

CALL FOR PAPERS

Textile Special Issue on DUST

Textile: The Journal of Cloth and Culture is proposing a special issue on "Dust," to be edited by Pennina Barnett (Goldsmiths College, University of London, UK), Catherine Harper (University of Brighton, UK) and Deborah Valoma (California College of the Arts, San Francisco, USA). The topic can be interpreted literally, metaphorically or conceptually to include, among other things, notions of invisibility, disintegration, insignificance and dispersal. We welcome proposals from researchers across disciplines. This issue will be published in 2009. We are working ahead to give writers plenty of time to work up proposals and to develop papers of up to 5,000 words in length.

If you would like to submit a paper, please submit an abstract of up to 500 words (with images if appropriate) to one of the DUST special issue editors listed below. Please feel free to contact us for further information.

DEADLINE FOR ABSTRACT SUBMISSION: 1 September 2008

CONTACT:
Pennina Barnett: p.barnett@gold.ac.uk
Catherine Harper: Catherine.Harper@brighton.ac.uk
Deborah Valoma: dvaloma@cca.edu

EDITED BY
LINDA WELTERS
ABBY LILLETHUN

The Fashion Reader

FOR YOUR BOOKSHELF
THIS SEASON'S FASHION ESSENTIAL

Designed for students, scholars, and anyone interested in contemporary fashion, *The Fashion Reader* brings together the key writings on the subject, covering the history, culture, and business of fashion.

NEW! February 2007 • 480pp • 60 bw illus **Paperback £19.99 / US$34.95**

order online at www.bergpublishers.com

Patched, Louse-ridden, Tattered: Clean and Dirty Clothes

Abstract

"Patched, louse-ridden, tattered—clean, beautiful, gem." As children we recited this rhyme in Norwegian: "Lappete, lusete, fillete—ren, pen, edelsten," as we picked petal after petal from a daisy. All the words can be understood as descriptions of the child's future clothes. Clean is the turning point in the rhyme. Clean is thus seen as the first step on the way towards the gem, and it conveys here the same meaning as in the saying "whole and clean is the greatest finery." Both emphasize clean clothes as crucial to the judgment of a person's appearance.

In the world of fashion it has been alleged that "anything goes." This is probably true if we restrict "anything" to small variations in the look, decor, color, and style of clothes. However, our way of dressing also depends on more absolute norms.

This article explores the norms that deal with the relationship between clean and dirty clothes. Despite the fact that there is abundant research on cleanliness and laundering on the one hand, and clothes and clothes habits on the other, there are few points of intersection between the two fields. The article is an attempt at seeing these two themes in conjunction. It investigates how clothes, by being kept clean, make bodies socially acceptable. The article looks at how the demand for cleanliness varies in relation to age, gender, and class, and compares these demands to what we know about decency.

Keywords: dress, cleanliness, laundering, decency, clothes habits, body

The article and all quotations from Norwegian publications are translated by Stig Erik Sørheim.

INGUN GRIMSTAD KLEPP
Ingun Grimstad Klepp has a PhD in ethnology and is Head of Research at the National Institute for Consumer Research, Norway. She wrote her MA and PhD on leisure time and outdoor life in ethnology at the University of Oslo. Her current field of research is clothing and housework.

Patched, Louse-ridden, Tattered: Clean and Dirty Clothes

"Patched, louse-ridden, tattered—clean, beautiful, gem." As children we recited this rhyme in Norwegian: "Lappete, lusete, fillete—ren, pen, edelsten" as we picked petal after petal from a daisy. The word on the last petal would indicate our future. The first five words are all to do with a person's appearance and several are explicitly about clothes. The gem comes as a surprising ending—incredible, almost unachievable wealth. All the words can be understood as descriptions of a child's future clothes. In this case, the gem will represent luxuriously decorated clothes like the Queen's coronation dress. It is, however, the little word "clean" that is interesting for our present purposes. Clean is the turning point in the rhyme from the negatively laden words: "patched, louse-ridden, tattered." Clean is thus seen as the first step on the way towards the gem. Consequently we can say that clean here conveys the same meaning as in the saying "hel og ren er største stasen"—"whole and clean is the greatest finery" (Figure 1).[1] Both emphasize clean clothes as crucial to the judgment of a person's character and status.

Since the 1990s in the world of fashion it has been alleged that "anything goes." This is probably true if we restrict "anything" to small variations in the look, decor, color, and style of clothes. However, our way of dressing also depends on more absolute norms.

In this article I wish to explore the norms that deal with the relationship between clean and dirty clothes. I will be looking at Norwegian literature on etiquette, earlier research and at empirical material about habits in clothing and laundering in Norway.[2] Despite the fact that there is abundant research on cleanliness and laundering on the one hand, and clothes and clothes habits on the other, there have been few attempts at seeing these two fields in conjunction. This article is such an attempt. I will investigate how clothes by being kept clean make bodies socially acceptable. I will limit myself here to looking at how the demand for cleanliness varies in relation to age, gender, and class, and at the same time I compare this to what we know about decency. Obviously, this question is too complex to go into detail here.

Ways of Understanding Cleanliness

The central point of reference in research on cleanliness is Mary Douglas's theory on dirt as matter out of place. "There is no such thing as absolute dirt" (Douglas 1984: 66), she wrote and argued that dirt is the result of a system of classification. Thereby she made

Velholdthed, er Betingelsen for Velklædthed.

Figure 1
"Well-kept is the condition for well-dressed." Drawing by Ebba Schultz in Stoumann (1938).

the clean and the dirty cultural constructs, which are suitable objects for cultural and social studies.

In the research on cleanliness Leach's taboo theory, Elias's civilization theory, and Foucault's perspective on power have been sources of inspiration. This is true for central studies like *Den kultiverade människan* (*Cultured Man*), which the ethnologists Jonas Frykman and Orvar wrote in 1979 (Frykman and Löfgren 1979), and *Lys, luft og renlighet, den moderne socialhygienens fødsel* (*Light, Air and Cleanliness, the Birth of the Modern Social Hygiene*) by the Danish historians of ideas Lars-Henrik Schmidt and Jens Erik Kristensen (Schmidt and Kristensen 1986). In the wake of these studies we find a rich variety of studies on hygiene-historical topics like culture and class struggle. The fight against dirt, disorder, bad manners, and bacteria is not only understood as a way to promote people's health, but also as a way of advancing the regulated, modern, bourgeois society. Several studies on the history of mentality give insight into the changes that occur over time. Particularly relevant to this article are *Aroma: The Cultural History of Smell* (Classen *et al.* 1994) and *Concepts of Cleanliness: Changing Attitudes in France since the Middle Ages* (Vigarello 1998).

Another perspective on cleanliness can be found in research on housework. The practical consequences of changed standards of cleanliness have been studied in this field. Particularly the relationship between time spent on housework and technology, and technology and practice have been investigated (Klepp 2003b; Shove 2003b). Much of this research neglected to reflect on cleanliness. It has considered the goal—clean clothes—as constant and unchanging, while technology and the structuring of work have undergone changes. One researcher who has discussed the goal of laundering is the famous Norwegian cultural and social scientist at the end of the nineteenth century, Eilert Sundt. His book, which was first published in 1869, is a study on cleanliness in the Norwegian countryside. He summarizes his arguments concerning cleanliness in this way:

> ... cleaning and decoration for the weekend is done for God and also for dinner parties and other social gatherings for the sake of the visitors, and, additionally, sometimes between such occasions or in everyday life in order not to be distressed too much by dirt and dust. (Sundt 1975: 66)

In addition to the weekly cleaning for the sake of God, there is cleaning in preparation for the big church festivals (Sundt 1975: 68). Sundt argues, then, that cleanliness has had three reasons: religious, social, and practical. He sees the religious reasons for cleanliness as older than Christianity.

In later years, several researchers have been interested in the goal of laundering. Lydia Martens has looked at the representation of domestic practice in the magazine *Good Housekeeping* after 1951 (Martens *et al.* 2003). Elizabeth Shove tries to identify the mechanisms that change what we at any given time conceive as a necessary and general standard of cleanliness. She sees morals, technology, and practice in conjunction. Rather than being a predefined goal or something that people strive to achieve, cleanliness is best understood as the outcome of whatever it is that people do in its name (Shove 2003). In this way cleanliness is associated more closely with practice. Cleanliness can be measured as absence of dirt and bacteria, but also as a cultural category. In line with the attempts at crossing the divides between the natural and social sciences there are also in this field researchers who look at the conjunctions between these two fields (Latour 1998; Shove 2003).

The large-scale hygiene project that washed Europe into modern times from the end of the nineteenth century and some way into the twentieth century can be seen as successful in two respects. It contributed towards eliminating large infectious mass diseases and it changed the understanding of the importance of cleanliness. What at the beginning of the twentieth century were introduced through instructions and control have become personal proclivities. Today everyone is capable of governing oneself (Foucault and Gordon 1980). Shove emphasizes that well-being has been given a more central place in our culture. It is referred to as something that should be universal and not something that is specific to time and place (Shove 2003). The increased importance of well-being and the increased emphasis on clothes free from body odors may be interpreted as showing that hygiene rules are transformed to bodily inclinations and aesthetic evaluations. They have had an independent existence, as Goffman argues (Goffman 1984), and need no longer be validated by questions of hygiene (Klepp 2006). These are examples of how the rules governing appearance are not just accidental and external, but also emergent forms of discipline and power. An investigation of the variations in these rules can thereby also be used to disclose these power structures.

Clothes as the Border between Clean and Dirty

Clothes can protect the surroundings from the body's impurities, or conversely protect the body from the surroundings. I will return to these two possibilities, but first I would like to point out that both of these perspectives build on a tradition where clothes are studied in relation to the body.

Kropp og klær (*Body and Clothes*) is the title of Broby-Johansen's book from 1923 (Broby-Johansen 1953). In this study, he insists that clothes should be studied in connection with the body. His book did not really have any followers, even though it was widely read in Scandinavia. Only in the 1980s did this perspective become important in clothes studies, at least as a conscious theoretical standpoint. It was pointed out that one of the radical aspects of seeing body and clothing in conjunction was that it broke down the distinction between nature and culture (Wilson 1985). The methodological and theoretical challenges this perspective creates are still not fully developed. One researcher who has worked with these issues is the sociologist Joanne Entwistle. She emphasizes that clothes exist at the body's limit towards the world; they therefore constitute a border between the individual and society. The function of clothes is to make the body accepted in the different social situations we find ourselves in (Entwistle 2000). How much is demanded from clothes, or how strict the clothes norms are, depends both on how much the body is subject to taboos and on the social situation.

Appearing in a public place without clothes is not permitted, neither socially nor legally. Decency has been discussed in clothes studies and some regard this as the primary function of clothes. We know quite a bit about the way clothes cover and reveal the body in connection with different cultures, gender, occasions, religions, and in time. In the Western tradition, nudity represents sin, shame as well as evil, but at the same time the naked body, and particularly the female body, has been worshipped for its beauty and natural innocence. Nevertheless, the erotic aspect of the nudity is always present (Hollander 2005: 84). More than hiding the body's gender, clothes will often accentuate and direct attention to the parts that should be covered. Thus, decency is not only a matter of the quantity of naked skin, but also of how the clothes cover or reveal the body, and how explicitly they relate to eroticism.

Douglas is known for arguing that not only is the body itself tabooed, but to an even greater extent the body's secretions (Douglas 1984). In Sundt, too, there are detailed descriptions of taboos and rituals connected with human waste in the form of clipped nails, hair, teeth, and washing water. The purpose of these customs is to render the waste harmless. Usually, this was done with fire. If it was not done, there was a notion that evil could employ the waste in its service. A famous example is the boat *Naglfar*, which was built from unburnt nail clippings. This boat will appear shortly before the end of the world (Sundt 1975: 59). Not only nail, hair, and beard clippings, but all bodily secretions are culturally problematic: urine, sweat, mucus, tears, mother's milk, menstruation blood, feces, discharges, pus, dandruff, and semen. Despite our advanced body techniques, clothes will inevitably be contaminated in contact with these substances (Mauss 1979). Thus, the clothes' function as a boundary is not independent of the way they are kept clean, in the sense that the remains of the body's impressions on the clothes are removed. To maintain a clear boundary we must not only have clothes, but also wash them (Klepp 2003b, 2005). Not everything is permitted here either.

One of the most fundamental functions of dress is to protect the body against the surroundings. This is most evident in armor, space suits, diving suits or clothes for use in extreme temperatures, but this aspect is also present in clothes in general. Dirt from the surroundings is one of several possible influences that the clothes should protect us from. In addition to the fact that clothes protect the body, a number of garments protect the clothes underneath against various types of dirt: aprons, overcoats, spats, sleeve protectors, etc.

If we look at the history of dress, the emphasis on these two aspects has varied. Georges Vigarello (1998) has pointed out that the practice of wearing separate layers of clothing and distinguishing between under- and outerwear dates back to the thirteenth century. In the Middle Ages, shirts of linen were thought of as a protective second skin, a line of defense against external vapors. This kind of underwear had the dual function of excluding unwanted influences from the outside and of mopping up the outpourings of the body (Shove 2003: 124). This function was not dependent on washing the body, rather the shirt was perceived as a sponge that absorbed impurities and thus kept the body clean.

The shirt was originally an undergarment hidden under other clothes. In the second half of the fifteenth century, shirt collars and sleeves became more and more visible, and thereby became subject to public judgment. The importance of collars and sleeves grew, and apparels were increasingly marked by the contrasts between the heavier fabrics in clothes and the often very thin, lacy, and white collars and sleeves. These visible parts of undergarments were important both aesthetically and, not least, symbolically by revealing what was hidden. The white shirt parts became the visible sign of bodily cleanliness as well as the cleanliness of clothes (Vigarello 1998). This is still a significant aspect of the use of shirts (Pettersen 2004).

Even if the habit of wearing different layers of clothes with different meanings continues to structure the symbolic meaning and organization of clothing and laundry today, it is also one of the factors that has changed since the mid-twentieth century. If we look at stability first, it is most evident in traditional clothes concepts, such as the man's suit, but is most conspicuous in the case of women's clothes (Klepp 2005).

From the 1950s and onwards the focus on dirt as something external (stains, dust, filth) has been weakened compared to the focus on dirt that comes from within (body oils, sweat). Consequently, protective pieces of clothing, such as aprons, are no longer meaningful and have gone out of daily use (Sandvik 1998). This change is closely related to the increased emphasis on odor rather than visual (or invisible) purity (Klepp 2005). Accordingly, it is completely unacceptable to put on clean clothes without washing first. However, the demand that the laundry is whiter than white, and that clothes are completely spotless is no longer as absolute.

Formulating a Clothes Norm

In the literature on fashion, clothes, and clothes habits the demand for cleanliness is not an issue that is treated explicitly or at length. One of the few places where it is mentioned is *The Language of Clothes*, but even here only briefly and introductorily. Lurie writes that cleanliness "is usually regarded as a sign of respectability or at least of self-respect" (Lurie 1981: 13). On the other hand, shabbily dressed people are "more apt to be treated shabbily" (Lurie 1981: 14). These aspects of cleanliness are central for the Salvation Army under the motto *Soap*, which, together with *Soup* and *Salvation*, forms the basis for their work. To give people clean clothes is to return dignity to them (Larssen and Bry 2002). The close connection between missionary work and soap does not only have positive sides. Colonies were established as markets for European products, and soap was an important element in incorporating new peoples into a civilized and urban world (Flikke 2005).

The etiquette literature gives direct advice for dressing and, not surprisingly, cleanliness is an important topic. In Norway the book *Skikk og bruk* (*Etiquette and Manners*) published by Capellen in 1960 occupies a central role in this genre (Brøgger 1960). The chapter "Kropp og klær" ("Body and Clothing") opens with four basic rules. In the first two, cleanliness is a major point, first in relation to the body and then to clothes.

> 1. The whole body from the head to the feet and the tips of your fingers must be kept clean and free from unpleasant smells ...
> 2. Clothes must be clean, proper and well-kept, and one has to be dressed appropriately for the occasion. (Brøgger 1960: 87)

Then there is a rule for language and manners. The next edition includes "twelve absolute demands" divided between demands on men and demands on women. All the demands, twenty-four in all, have to do with cleanliness and properness:

> *No half-dirty collars, trousers or sweaters!*
> *No stained, unaired, unpressed clothes!*
> *No dirty collar and dirty shirt!*
> *No unwashed socks! etc.*
> (Brøgger 1960: 88)

From the end of the 1970s and onwards to the present day, much of this has become self-evident and therefore not something that is treated directly in writing. Still, cleanliness for body and clothes is an issue. In one of the latest books I have looked at, showing up "filthy" comes second on the list of the worst things a guest can do (Larssen and Bry 2002).

In the same way as in the editions of *Skikk og bruk* (*Etiquette and Manners*), the demands concerning clean clothes are very prominent in the empirical material. "I told my children that whatever people might criticize them for, let nobody say that they are not clean or that their clothes are dirty" (NEG190k32b). "People who smell or look unkempt are the worst" (NEG190k66). As in *Skikk og bruk* (*Etiquette and Manners*) this is formulated as an absolute demand. If it is broken, that is "the worst" one can do. Clean clothes are important for oneself and in relation to others: "It is important to have clean clothes. Besides, it is uncomfortable to walk around feeling that a piece of clothing is dirty and be afraid that you smell of sweat" (NEG190k59a). As we see, these two aspects of cleanliness are closely connected. Clothes must be clean in order for people to feel good, but this form of well-being is closely associated with the judgment of others.

It's just the way it has become, that it's embarrassing, in fact disgraceful to look dirty. To go two days in the same blouse or t-shirt, no, that's just not something we do. 'Cause then we feel that people talk behind our backs! (NEG190k57b)

Both the etiquette literature and the empirical material show a change. This change can be formulated as a personal development. "Earlier I was careful that my clothes should be clean all the time. Afraid to smell of sweat" (NEG190k80). But this can also be formulated as a difference between generations. "Earlier cleanliness was something that made you a good or a bad person—I still have many of my mother's comments about this in the back of my head. I am glad it's not like that, because that's just ornamental" (NEG190k57a). Such statements must be seen in light of the fact that the general frequency of washing today is much higher than twenty, forty or sixty years ago, both as regards the body and clothes. It is no longer necessary to formulate the demand for cleanliness because to be clean has become internalized to the extent that it has become second nature. The possibility of achieving this is completely different. "Old people took pride in keeping their clothes proper whenever possible" (NEG190k29b). People still take pride in keeping clothes clean (Klepp 2005), but dirty clothes do not separate the poor from the rich in today's Norway. In these formulations of the norm we have been considering this far, the demands have been presented as general and absolute. In practice, however, there are variations concerning what is considered clean and how dirt is judged. In the following, I will try to explore such variations and, simultaneously, compare them with variations in the demand for decency. I will limit the discussion to material from Norway from recent times and in relation to age, gender, and class. This does not mean that other perspectives are less interesting. I could have chosen to study the questions in relation to different occasions and pieces of clothing,[3] diachronically,[4] in different settings or related to different religions,[5] just to mention a few possibilities.

Variations in a Clothes Norm: Age

How much of the body that at any given time has to be covered by clothes varies with age. In Norway it has been customary to hang pictures of the family's naked baby in the living room. Similar pictures of older children, not to mention older relatives, would be unthinkable. As the child grows, the lower abdomen must be covered in public. Young people and young adults may dress more provocatively and show more skin than adults. Elderly people must pay special attention and cover their bodies more than younger people (Lurie 1981; Storm-Mathisen and Klepp 2005: 50). Since youth fashion has become the ideal we can observe mature adults dressed as teenagers, but the bare midriffs and the very short skirts are generally the prerogative of young people. What, then, about the demand for cleanliness? Does it follow the same pattern where the body seems to become more strongly tabooed with age?

Most people agree that children produce a lot of laundry. The infant soils his/her clothes from within. "The most characteristic trait of the infant is its inability to keep dry and free from excrements" (Wintzell 1972: 28). As soon as the child begins to eat and move about, it also dirties him/herself from the outside. From the 1950s and onwards, the child's ability to dirty and wear out clothes is described as a fact of life that parents have to deal with (Torell 2003). A good, Nordic childhood is a childhood filled with play and activity, indoors and not least outdoors, where the child is in close contact with snow and ice, dirt and mud, paint, clay, etc. (Figure 2). "Children should be allowed to get dirty" (Statens Institutt for Forbruksforskning 1977: 14), as it says in a brochure about good children's clothes. Thus, one might suspect that dirty children have a positive value as happy and healthy children. That may well be the case, but at the same time, children are a showcase for the family's wealth and success, and there are situations where it is strongly emphasized that children should be clean.

Figure 2
Outdoor activities have great importance in a Norwegian childhood. Children shall have the liberty to run free and therefore also get dirty. It is the responsibility of mothers with the help of washing machines and washing powder to ensure that children still go out clean every day. Advertisement for Blenda from 2006 with the slogan: "even the most dirty children have sensitive skins … That is why Blenda Sensitiv exists." The frequent washing of children's clothes is hence seen as a potential danger to the children's skins.

School is one of the arenas that are most frequently mentioned as an example of a place where clean clothes are important (Figure 3). In statements such as "I prided myself on making sure that the children always had clean clothes, both at home and at school" (NEG190k24), the high standard is not that the children were clean at school—most people would aim for that—but that they also should be clean at home. Nobody has mentioned kindergarten in connection with demands of clean clothes; on the contrary, there are statements indicating that it does not matter if the kindergarten clothes have stains. For older people, contact with the health services is an example of a situation where clean clothes are particularly important. Both schools and health services played

Figure 3
We do not have school uniforms in Norway, but pupils must still have clean and nice clothes. This is particularly important on special days in school such as May 17 (the Norwegian national day) and the first day of school. Schoolgirl in 1945. Privately owned photo.

a central role in the introduction of the new hygienic standard. Schools had an important role in monitoring family hygiene. The emphasis on schools as an arena where clean clothes are particularly important is probably associated with this function. We see how meanings associated with everyday practices live on long after changes occur on a political or administrative level. The power once inherent in school and health-care institutions has been transformed into aesthetic evaluations that today have taken on a life of their own, and that is why it is important to be clean when meeting these institutions.

The mother who took such pride in her clean children goes on to write that her children never were scolded if they got dirty, "after all that was part of life" (NEG190k24). Her standards for their cleanliness should not inhibit their play. Thus, she is aware that clean children could also be perceived as passive, inhibited, and unhealthy children. She solved the contradiction created by the two opposing norms by washing and mending without complaints. She (and her washing machine) was the one who should carry the burden, not the children. This self-imposed sacrifice is not particularly associated with this woman's generation (Miller 1998). Rather, it seems that the standard has been raised in that "nice and clean" clothes today are not only interpreted as whole and spotless, but as newly washed. "My mother says that I wash the clothes before I need to, that I create too much work for myself. But I really want the kids to smell good and have clean clothes" (NEG190k61a).

During adolescence, children get or take more responsibility for their own hygiene and to a certain extent also for the cleanness of their clothes. The question then arises whether the standards they set for themselves are in accordance with those of their mothers.[6] In the empirical data most of the information on this issue is in connection with the shower and cleaning habits of young boys. The narrative that is repeated tells us that the boys wash themselves and their clothes more often than their mothers feel is required. However, the mothers prefer this rather than a situation where the boys wash too little. "My kids are grown now, but I remember very well how it was to keep them whole and clean when they were little" (NEG190k17a). One of them was "special when it came to changing his shirts. But I never complained because it was much better that he changed 'too often' than too little" (NEG190k7a).

What, then, about the demands for cleanliness in adults? In data material on clothes habits among women around forty years of age it appears that many of the women feel that their position at work and with the family requires more proper clothes than they allowed themselves to wear as students and young adults. It also demands that the clothes should be cleaner, have fewer stains and wrinkles than before (Klepp 2001). The same is found, but for both sexes, in a postgraduate thesis about the transition from student life to work life. Here the subject is discussed more in terms of different styles than as standards of cleanliness *per se*. In the description of different styles, expressions such as "the pants are like beginning to get baggy at the knees," "careless trend," "untidy clothes" are used on the one hand and "neat, nice and impeccable" and "correct" on the other (Kjepso 1999).

There is little literature on older people's clothes. In the empirical material on laundry, we find statements like, "older people with shabby clothes are unpleasant" (NEG190k23a) and "I am disgusted with old people who smell unwashed" (NEG109k63a). However, it is not easy to say whether it is particularly objectionable that elderly people have unwashed clothes, or whether this rather refers to the fact that many old people rarely wash their clothes. Laundry frequency among elderly people is lower than among the population as a whole (Arild *et al*. 2003). This is not surprising since daily routines are tenacious structures that change slowly, even when cleaning routines have been intensified during their lifetime, particularly with regard to the body and clothes.

The evaluation of body odor changes with age. It is customary to feel that babies smell very good and that children smell good when they are clean. Teenagers and adults should hide their body odor. But the elderly are the worst. As the quote above shows, their body odor is "disgusting." If we think of body odor as sexual communication (Fyrand 2002), this fits particularly well with the view of the relationship between age and sexuality in general (Storm-Mathisen and Klepp 2005).

Variations in standards of cleanliness and the perception of body odor seem to follow the same pattern as the requirements for clothes to cover the body. The baby's body is pure and innocent both as odor and in the visual sense, but later in life it is more and more important to keep the clothes clean and hide the body and its odor.

Variations in a Clothes Norm: Gender

The relationship between gender and the standards of decency is a major issue in the study of clothes. And in general, gender in this connection means women. It is the female body that is the object of most of the fuss surrounding nudity. Female nudity is a crucial matter in a society that seems to make woman embody sex itself. Throughout history different parts of the female body had to be hidden, head and hair, ankles and knees, etc. The fuss over Muslim women's head veil in modern Western societies also indicates that the norms not only regulate how much of the female body should be covered, but also the reverse, how much should be shown. Paradoxically, in today's dress norms women's bodies on the one hand should be more covered than men's bodies, for instance, it is acceptable for men to have a bare upper body in a number of situations where it is not permitted for women. On the other hand, women's bodies are generally much more undressed than men's, and uncovered female bodies are seen in a number of situations. The image of feminine desirability is the modern mass consumer culture's most powerful icon (De Grazia and Furlough 2005). To desire the fashionable, purchasable woman-as-thing is to desire exchange value itself. According to Walter Benjamin, this is the very essence of capitalism (De Grazia and Furlough 2005).

Women's clothes are washed more frequently than men's. This difference has been documented in Norway since the 1950s (Jagmann 1959). Today the biggest difference is found for underwear, where 59 percent of the men and 94 percent of the women say that they change every day. For socks the corresponding figures are 56 percent for men and 71 percent for women (Klepp 2003b: Appendix 1). There is no reason to believe that this is because men's socks get less dirty than women's. Women do most of the laundry work in Norway (SSB 2002). This is in no way a recent development. Sundt describes how a woman is brought into disrepute if a man in her household is uncleanly. An old adage states that "A good wife can make a good husband, but a good husband cannot make a good wife" (NEG169k22). Thus, when men's clothes are washed less frequently, there is reason to believe that it is not just due to a difference in how the two sexes perceive cleanliness, but just as much an expression of what women feel that the standards should be. Women accept lower laundry frequency for men's clothes, but not necessarily the standards that men themselves set. "The man of the house thinks the clothes are washed too often and wears them until they smell. I have to check!" (NEG190k63a). On the contrary, they engage in extensive investigative sniffing and in various ways second-guess both their husband's and other family members' standards (Klepp 2005).

Teaching children cleanliness is described very differently depending on the gender of the child. It is portrayed as a feat to have raised a child into a cleanly man.

I hope I have taught my two sons about personal hygiene. As far as I can tell, they shower almost more than me, and they are meticulous about their clothes. They make sure to shave and keep their hair well groomed. (NEG190k30a)

There are no corresponding descriptions of daughters in the examined material. None of the women writes that they have not succeeded in teaching their sons cleanliness but, in the way they describe it, it is evident that this possibility exists in the women's mind.

Women's and men's body odors are judged differently (Classen et al. 1994; Maartmann 1998). For example, this was one of the arguments against women's entry into endurance sports like cross-country skiing and running. In the literature on etiquette and conduct, women's cleanliness is described differently than men's. Statements like "Body odor is equally wrong in a man as in a woman" (Brøgger 1960: 183), are more a confirmation of this than anything else. Cleanliness is one of the feminine virtues, but at the same time it is also more of a virtue of necessity, according to this literature. Women's body odor is more unpleasant, not to mention more disgraceful. The anthropologist Jorunn Solheim suggests one possible explanation for this (Solheim 1998). She discusses how thoughts about pollution in many cultures have a primary reference to women. She finds the explanation for this in the fact that women's bodies are more open and lack the clear definition of the male body. The male body is more closed and self contained, and therefore *cleaner*. In contrast to the situation for men, it takes more than soap and water to make a dirty woman clean. The assessment of women's body odor is closely related to her sexual experience. The smell of young girls, especially virgins, is associated with wild flowers, while in several languages the term for whore is derived from the word *putrid* (Classen et al. 1994).

For men, the demands for clean clothes are particularly connected with one item of clothing: the shirt. As we saw, this was a separate subsection in *Skikk og bruk* (*Etiquette and Conduct*). It is portrayed in a similar manner in other books on etiquette. "The accessory is an impeccable white shirt" (Bagge-Skarheim and Olaussen 1965: 39). The conspicuously clean and ironed shirt in a sense guarantees that the man as a whole stays within the norms that are set (Pettersen 2004).

Men's other clothes are not subject to the same attention. In fact, white-collar workers' clothes are washed—or dry-cleaned—less frequently than other equivalent clothes. A pair of jeans is washed after a couple of days' use (Arild et al. 2003), while suit pants are very rarely washed or dry-cleaned. There is not much difference between the two pieces of clothing in terms of closeness to the body (Klepp 2003b).

In clear contrast to the white-collar profession, in manual male jobs clean clothes have a more ambiguous status. Lurie describes this as a characteristic of rural and small towns generally, as a "dislike of the persons whose clothes are too clean, slick and smooth. She—and, less often, he—is suspected of being untrustworthy, a smoothie or a city slicker" (Lurie 1981: 13). As Lurie also suggests, this is first and foremost the case for men. When women entered the trades and industries, dirt was regarded as a problem. This was solved by using a uniform at work, which was then exchanged for other clothes at the end of the workday. This practice has also become common among men (Steele 1989).

The ambiguous status of clean clothes among men, along with men's infrequent changes of clothes and lack of laundry skills, are a fertile area within the comic genre (Figure 4). The following story about a trip to the bank illustrates men's and women's differing views on clean work clothes.

The blacksmith made ready to go as he was. His wife did not approve and told him that there was no sense in going to the bank in those dirty pants. The blacksmith answered: "Oh yeah, it is in these pants that I make a penny." (NEG190m20)

Dirty clothes represent proper, honest work. In contrast, a man with too clean clothes may be ridiculed. "I know that my husband is meticulous about whole and clean clothes. When he started his new job he had to wear clean clothes, and they called him *lompen*" (NEG190k32a).[7] Similar ridicule of a woman with clean clothes is unthinkable. In contrast to the case for men, there is a total absence of good stories about women and dirty clothes, and about women and laundry. It seems that the requirement of cleanliness is so absolute that it is not funny.

The ridicule of men who are overly concerned with their outward appearance is not a recent phenomenon. In satirical drawings from the eighteenth century the rough, unaffected, masculine man is contrasted with a refined, effeminate man. There is no doubt whom the joke is on (Claro 2005). Ever since the eighteenth century a modest masculinity has legitimized political power (De Grazia and Furlough 2005).

I previously have discussed the relationship between clean clothes and feminine purity in the metaphorical sense (Klepp 2005). In that context I discussed the demand on variation, i.e. not wearing the same clothes several days in a row or on several occasions can be understood as a way to visualize an otherwise invisible purity. In this way, clothes are not only spotless and odorless, but the variation shows that they are frequently changed (and thus potentially washed). The demand on variation is much stronger for women than for men.

Figure 4
Clothes must be clean, but not always. Gardening is an occasion where clean clothes are not that important. This picture from 1929 is meant to be funny. The conspicuously clean clothes appear comical in certain situations. The man dressed wholly in white gives associations to something dandyish and vain, miles away from cute and delicate innocence. Both too clean men and too clean clothes can be ridiculous. Photo from private collection.

The differences in the standards of purity for the two sexes also show in the meaning that is attached to entirely white clothes. To women white clothes connote virginity, as in a wedding dress (Kjellberg 1991), but also more generally (Figure 5). Men in white are sexually suspect. They appear affected, dandyish or eccentric (Klepp 2004) (Figure 4).

The relationship between decency and occasion is an extensive topic in etiquette literature and clothes studies. The female body must be covered in situations where she needs to appear serious, responsible, and professional (Steele 1989). On the other hand, a festive occasion requires a more undressed woman. For men it is the other way around, the more festive the occasion, the more dressed he is, and similarly he wears more clothes on formal occasions. These observations may well be seen in conjunction. If fewer, thinner and smaller items of clothing are left to hide the body and its odor, strict demands must be placed on their purity in order to maintain the boundary between the body and the world. The extensive use of perfume on the undressed female body supports this interpretation. But in this case perfume cannot be interpreted exclusively as a strategy to attract men, but also as a shield against intimacy.[8] The nudity that fills our public space is a particular form of polished and flawless nudity that does not reveal the body's secretions and odors, nor, ideally, wrinkles and hair (Isaksen 2002).

Even though the use of some cosmetic products is increasing among men, the smell of perfume is first and foremost associated with women. Men have an ambiguous relationship to this. In the most common interpretation women use perfume to attract men, and thus to be the chosen one. But as pointed out in *Aroma: The Cultural History of Smell* (Classen et al. 1994: 163), "At the same time as they attempt to enhance their attractiveness, they surround themselves with an aura of foolishness. No sensible person (i.e. man) would wear such nonsense."

The relationship between the demands on purity of clothes and sex is a complex field where much work remains to be done. It seems that these norms do not conform to the same pattern as those connected with decency. In the case of decency we found that the female body was both more tabooed and at the same time the object of much greater aesthetic attention. In many situations it must and should be uncovered. With regard to men the norms are clearer and more absolute. However, in the case of purity the norms are more complex for men. Dirty clothes, and particularly a dirty white shirt, will reduce a man's credibility, however, in some situations dirt has a value. In these cases dirty clothes are interpreted as a sign of honesty, masculinity, and participation in "proper work."

Figure 5
Bride in white strapless dress; groom in shirt, vest, and jacket. The use of white wedding dresses dates back to around 1830. But only in the second half of the twentieth century did this attain a symbolic significance as the sign of the bride's virginity. The undressed woman and the dressed man mark big occasions. Famefotografene Tønsberg, Jostein Marvik 1995. Private collection.

Women should always be clean. It is possible that this is only on the surface and may be explained by the fact that it is much harder to provide material about female impurity. In any case, common to the norms about purity and decency is the fact that the female body and its odors are the most problematic, while men are both more natural and less interesting.

Variations in a Clothes Norm: From Class to Style

What do we know about decency in a class perspective? Clearly this is a complex phenomenon. Throughout history the upper class has been more dressed and buttoned up than their sisters and brothers among the common people. In paintings, for instance, there are many lightly dressed gypsy girls and peasant maids, not to speak of naked savages. For as Hollander writes, "The more significant clothing is, the more meaning attaches to its absence, and the more awareness is generated about any relation between the two states" (Hollander 2005: 83). Jonas Frykman has thoroughly described the different meanings of nudity among Swedish peasants and bourgeoisie in Sweden at the end of the nineteenth century (Frykman and Löfgren 1979). Valerie Steele has analyzed office dress and shows how sexually provocative clothes characterize women in subordinate positions, while the professional career woman is characterized by her formal, buttoned-up suit (Steele 1989). However, it seems that this is changing, and today there are women who insist on both power and sexualized dress.

Today's most famous women, if not necessarily the richest, strut up and down Hollywood's red carpet far more undressed than what is generally accepted. This nakedness may be understood both as artistic license to exceed common norms, but also as the tendency of stage clothes to exaggerate.

Poverty smells in terms of difference—it is always the others who smell (Classen *et al.* 1994). But with regard to the relationship between rich and poor this has also been a reality. Keeping body and clothes clean is expensive and time consuming, and even more so in the past. As long as clean clothes were unattainable for those with limited means, conspicuously clean clothes were associated with prestige, particularly clothes that were time consuming to keep clean. White collars, chalk-white sports shoes, and white clothes in sports such as tennis, sailing, and polo may well be interpreted in this way (Schreier 1989) (Figure 6).

A few generations ago, Norway was one of the poorest countries in Europe. Most people had little surplus fat to boil soap from, little money to spend, and until the end of the Second World War they often did not have running water or bathrooms in the house. As the demands for washing the body and textiles became stricter from the end of the nineteenth century, particularly in the interwar period, cleanliness became an important distinction between people. This distinction was still significant in the 1960s and 1970s. "It is easier to become friends with someone who's clean" (NEG190k61b) writes a woman born in 1961, and she goes on to

Figure 6
White is expensive to keep clean. This is probably part of the reason why white dominates in prestigious sports like polo, tennis, and sailing.

describe her childhood without running water in the house. "But I remember I had to wash carefully!" with a washbasin and a rag. She does not think that she smelled herself, "but I remember homes where it smelled like cowshed all over the place—and that smell sticks!" (NEG190k61b). Perhaps it was children from homes like these who did not make friends so easily? She does not pursue this further. But it is clear that children from homes that did not have the wherewithal to implement the hygienic practices that the standards of the 1960s required could have a hard time. Without a bathroom and hot water even greater demands were placed on the responsible woman.

There are still poor people, but in Norway they are not distinguished by the lack of a bathroom, running water or other facilities for washing clothes. Rather, people with low incomes work harder than others to keep their clothes whole and clean, particularly for the children (Middleton et al. 1997; Rysst 2006). With the exception of special groups, such as street people, "whole and clean" is no longer a distinction between rich and poor. Today, unkempt children are more signals of lack of care than of poverty. This has opened up for the possibility that patched, tattered, and unclean (if not louse-ridden in the literal sense) could be picked up as a consciously chosen style. This kind of anti-fashion dates back to the hippies and "freaks" of the 1960s and 1970s, and can be seen as a rebellion against the cleanliness tyranny of the housewives (Schmidt and Kristensen 1986). This was also an important part of women's liberation in the 1970s, where strict cleanliness standards were interpreted as oppressive and unnecessary conventions (Døving and Klepp 2003).

Since then different types of anti-fashion have incorporated a more or less conscious use of seemingly dirty clothes. We see it in punk and in environmentalist style with extensive use of natural fabrics, work clothes, and elements of artifacts from oppressed population groups (Jacobson 1994). In these styles, dirty clothes are used partly as a general protest and to attract attention, but also as a more direct political message against society's great focus on cleanliness, appearance, and consumption (Wintzell 1985: 119).

Jeans producers quickly caught on to young people's way of individualizing the mass-produced. Jeans with ready-made patches and tatters were sold in the 1970s. Gradually, you could buy not only ready-worn and patched, but also seemingly dirty clothes. There is reason to believe that these elements carry different meanings, although to my knowledge this phenomenon has not yet been examined. The seemingly dirty clothes may be understood as reckless, tough, provoking or daring. There is little reason to think that the smell of unwashed clothes or bodies would have the same status, but nonetheless it is interesting that fashion has been able to pick up and transform something that originally was as stigmatizing as dirty clothes. This may be young people's way of creating a distinction from older people's use of jeans. In the same way as bare stomachs, dirt is less easily introduced into the ranks of the establishment. Generally, anti-fashion is a phenomenon that is considerably toned down in the transition to work life, with the exception of some liberal professions (Kjepso 1999).

To compare norms of decency and cleanliness with regard to class is to venture on thin ice, since the knowledge about both phenomena is relatively scarce.

Nevertheless, it seems that the norms conform to the same pattern even here. If we leave out sacred uncleanliness and focus on the last two centuries, it seems that strict demands on cleanliness and decency have been a characteristic of the upper class. This becomes less clear as we approach our own time. As a result of different styles and the opportunity of some high-status people to break with existing clothes norms, dress does not follow status the way it used to. With regard to dirty clothes this has been picked up as an aesthetic effect in anti-fashion, where rebellion and youth are central values. Still, it seems that anti-fashion is toned down in accordance with the demands that age, particularly in the sense of position, places on decent reliability. This type of decency requires both clean clothes and covering the parts of the body that are regarded as particularly sexually interesting.

The Greatest Finery

This analysis has shown that clothes norms connected with clean clothes are complex and vary with age, gender, and class. To some extent, these norms seem to conform to the norms connected with decency. This is understandable since both have to do with the way the body is made socially acceptable. The strength of the tabooing of the body and the importance of the social situation have significance for both areas. At the same time there are also differences between the norms. Schools and health-care institutions are particularly important with regard to cleanliness, but do not stand out with regard to decency. The cultural meaning of dirty men is complex, while a correspondingly paradoxical status is attached to the naked female body in our culture.

In the introduction, I wrote that I would discuss the meaning of clean clothes in relation to age, gender, and class, and not address other factors such as occasions, type of garment, etc. But as we have seen, these aspects have been touched upon in the process. In the discussion of age, school is an important arena with regard to children's clothes. Similarly, in the discussion of gender it was impossible to avoid a particular piece of clothing, namely, the shirt. The different aspects are of course not self-contained and independent, but deeply and intensely interwoven. To paint a fuller picture on the canvas that I have drawn up, it is necessary to use different approaches and focus both on the various aspects individually and on how they are interconnected.

In this article, I have in no way exhausted these subjects, neither in scope nor in depth. And I have not even touched upon the variation in types of dirt or where on the body it is found, just mentioned a few examples. Furthermore, I have just barely discussed the relationship between tabooing of visible dirt and stains, compared to smell. Nonetheless, the discussion has clearly shown that not everything goes, and certainly not everywhere for all people. Patched, louse-ridden, and tattered may be acceptable for rebellious youth, but the responsible adult must dress in clean clothes. And even the luster of the gem will be completely overshadowed if the clothes underneath are not clean. Today, just as in the past, whole and clean is the greatest finery. This survey has shown that the rules attached to the cleanliness of women's clothes are the strictest. While it is claimed that "anything goes," many people, particularly women, struggle to find something to wear (Klepp 2004; Miller 1998). Confronted with the lavish offerings of the clothes stores or our own crowded wardrobes, the problem is not to decide which of all these clothes we feel most like wearing. On the contrary, it seems that the problem for many people is to find something to wear that is not completely wrong, something they dare to wear, and something that does not attract unwanted attention. Many people know when something is wrong, but not what is right, and certainly not why. I believe that clothes studies can contribute to clarifying the unwritten norms that regulate our lives and contribute towards showing which ideologies and powers structures form the bases of these norms. Perhaps then it will be easier to make up our minds about them, whether to more easily comply with them or to reject them as irrelevant to our lives. Because it is certainly not up to the number of petals on a daisy to decide how we are going to dress.

Notes

1. This is a widely used expression in Norway. Eilert Sundt used it as a motto for his work on cleanliness in Norway towards the end of the nineteenth century. By calling attention to this popular saying he argued that there was a wish for neatness in the general public. There is something democratic about the thought that everyone through effort can wash his way to "the greatest finery" (Sundt 1975: 43).

2. The material consists of: (1) qualitative interviews with twenty-four women around the age of forty. The respondents, who were recruited from various regions in Norway, were interviewed individually. All of them were interviewed twice, first about the habits in clothing, and the follow-up interviews were concerned with the clothes the women had stopped wearing, and their discarded clothes (329 garments) were collected and registered. (2) Answers to a questionnaire on laundering compiled by the author in cooperation with NEG (Norwegian Ethnological Research). The material includes ninety-eight responses from Norwegian women and men. The responses are referred to with codes (NEG190k06) where NEG190 indicates the number NEG has assigned to this questionnaire and 06 is the year the informant is born (1906). "k" indicates woman and "m" man. (3) An analysis of written material from 1950 to 2003: thirty school textbooks used in Norwegian schools, fifty-eight laundry investigations and advice for laundering, fourteen books on etiquette, and finally seven

interviews on laundering. Further description of the material can be found in Klepp (2001, 2006) and in English in Klepp (2003a, 2005), Storm-Mathisen and Klepp (2002, 2005).
3. The dress worn in connection with the celebration of graduation from *videregående skole* (equiv. sixth-form), called *russedrakt*, is a piece of clothing, for which dirt and stains have a special significance. An unwritten rule says that this dress should not be washed during the weeks of celebration. The originally red (or blue) boilersuit-like piece of clothing attains its form through the owner's own decorations and greetings from friends written with Indian ink. Only through wear and tear and dirt indicating intense living does it receive its final and correct form (Hjemdahl 1999).
4. There are some studies that discuss changes in the perceptions of cleanliness over time. Broby-Johansen and a series of other dress historians discuss louse, dirt, and stench in the Renaissance and the Baroque periods (Broby-Johansen 1953: 146).
5. Christian hermits' holy uncleanliness is described in Endsjø (2002, 2003). From Africa today there are descriptions of creased and not newly washed and ironed used clothes as genuinely *salaula*, second-hand and not third-hand, i.e. not from dead African bodies (Hansen 2000: 173). Another study on African life compares clothes' function and the relationship between the body and clothes in the dress code of Christians, Muslims, and animists, and cleanliness is also considered (Andrewes 2005). Inspired by nuns, Christians speak of microbes and bacteria and cleanliness as a way to protect oneself against illness. This is incomprehensible to the animists. For them illness is an imbalance in the spiritual realm. For the Muslims cleanliness is part of their religious practice and leads to spiritual cleanliness (Andrewes 2005: 195–6).
6. Women's dominant position as clothes washers and, if men do the laundry, as responsible for the standards, makes the relationship to the father irrelevant in this connection (Klepp 2006; Kaufmann 1998).
7. *Lompen* means work clothes. In this context it is used as a nickname in an ironic sense.
8. In an article the Norwegian sociologist Hompland describes the smell of perfume "as the stench of women." He interprets this as unsuccessful communication, where the ladies try to please others, but instead pester their surroundings. My interpretation is the opposite of his. The stench is not there to attract men, but to keep others at a distance (Hompland 2005).

References

Andrewes, Janet. 2005. *Bodywork: Dress as Cultural Tool: Dress and Demeanor in the South of Senegal.* Leiden: Brill.

Arild, Anne-Helene et al. 2003. *An Investigation of Domestic Laundry in Europe: Habits, Hygiene and Technical Performance*. Oslo: Statens Institutt for Forbruksforskning.

Bagge-Skarheim, Randi and Jorunn Olaussen. 1965. *Vi ter og kler oss* [*How We Behave and Dress*]. Oslo: Elingaard brevskole.

Broby-Johansen, Rudolf. 1953[1923]. *Kropp og klær* [*Body and Clothes*]. Copenhagen: Tiden.

Brøgger, Waldemar (ed.). 1960. *Skikk og bruk* [*Etiquette and Manners*]. Oslo: J. W. Cappelens Forlag.

Claro, Daniel. 2005. "Historizing Masculine Appearance: John Chute and the Suits at the Vyne, 1740–76." *Fashion Theory* 9: 147–74.

Classen, Constance, David Howes and Anthony Synnott. 1994. *Aroma: The Cultural History of Smell*. London: Routledge.

De Grazia, Victoria and Ellen Furlough (eds). 2005. *The Sex of Things: Gender and Consumption in Historical Perspective*. Berkeley, CA: University of California Press.

Douglas, Mary. 1984. *Purity and Danger: An Analysis of the Concepts of Pollution and Taboo*. London: Ark Paperbacks.

Døving, Runar and Ingun Grimstad Klepp. 2003. "Hybelkaninenes erotiske bøtteballett" ["The Erotic Bucket Ballet of Dust Balls"]. *Prosa* 3. Oslo: Norsk faglitterær forfatter- og oversetterforening.

Endsjø, Dag Øistein. 2002. *The Body in the Periphery: Reading Athanasius' Vita Antonii from the Perspective of a Traditional Greek Woldview*. Oslo: Universitetet i Oslo.

Endsjø, Dag Øistein. 2003. *Parfyme, død og udødelighet* [*Perfume, Death and Immortality*]. Copenhagen: Institut for religionshistorie.

Entwistle, Joanne. 2000. *The Fashioned Body: Fashion, Dress, and Modern Social Theory*. Cambridge: Polity Press.

Flikke, Rune. 2005. "Såpe som politisk praksis og religiøs prosess i Sør-Afrika" ["Soap as Political Practice and Religious Process in South Africa"]. *Norsk antropologisk tidsskrift* 16: 152–62.

Foucault, Michel and Colin Gordon. 1980. *Power/Knowledge: Selected Interviews and Other Writings 1970–1997*. New York: Pantheon Books.

Frykman, Jonas and Orvar Löfgren. 1979. *Den kultiverade människan* [*Cultured Man*]. Stockholm: Liber Förlag.

Fyrand, Ole. 2002. *Berøring* [*Touch*]. Oslo: Pantagruel.

Goffman, Erving. 1984. *The Presentation of Self in Everyday Life*. London: Penguin Press.

Hansen, Karen Tranberg. 2000. *Salaula: The World of Secondhand Clothing and Zambia*. Chicago, IL: University of Chicago Press.

Hjemdahl, Anne-Sofie. 1999. *Kledd i russetid: En samtidsstudie av rødrussens klær* [*Dressed for Graduation Celebration: A Contemporary Study of the Clothes of Sixth-form Graduates*]. Oslo: A.-S. Hjemdahl.

Hollander, Anne. 2005. *Seeing through Clothes*. New York: Penguin Books.

Hompland, Andreas. 2005. "Stanken av damer: eit notat om ubehaget i den sensate kulturen: med noen metodologiske implikasjonar" ["The Stench of Ladies: A Note on Unpleasantness in the Present Culture: With Some Methodological Implications"]. *Sosiologi i dag* 36: 77–82.

Isaksen, Lise Widding. 2002. "Om angsten for de andres avsky" ["On the Angst for Other People's Disgust"]. In Trygve Wyller (ed.) *Skam. Perspektiver på skam, ære og skamløshet i det moderne* [*Shame. Perspectives on Shame, Honor and Shamelessness in Modernity*], pp. 213–43. Bergen: Fagbokforlaget.

Jacobson, Maja. 1994. *Kläder som språk och handling: om unga kvinnors användning av klädseln som kommunikations- och identitetsskapande medel* [*Clothes as Language and Act: On Young Women's Use of Dress as Communication- and Identity-forming Means*]. Stockholm: Carlsson.

Jagmann, Christian. 1959. *Klesvask; Familiens vasketøymengde* [*Laundering: The Family's Amount of Laundry*]. Stabekk: Statens Forsøksvirksomhet i Husstell.

Kaufmann, Jean-Claude. 1998. *Dirty Linen: Couples and Their Laundry*. London: Middlesex University Press.

Kjellberg, Anne. 1991. *Brudekjolen: Norske bryllupsmoter gjennom 400 år* [*The Wedding Dress: Norwegian Wedding Fashion through 400 Years*]. Oslo: Huitfeldt.

Kjepso, Helena. 1999. *Fra en tilknappet tidsalder til stipluralisme og kompleksitet: en studie av klesbruken på slutten av det 19 og 20 århundre* [*From a Buttoned-up Age to Pluralism and Complexity: A Study of Clothes Usage at the End of the 19th and 20th Century*]. Bergen: Universitetet i Bergen.

Klepp, Ingun Grimstad. 2001. *Hvorfor går klær ut av bruk?* [*Why Do Clothes Go out of Use?*]. Oslo: Statens Institutt for Forbruksforskning.

Klepp, Ingun Grimstad. 2003a. *Clothes and Cleanliness. Why We Still Spend as Much Time on Laundry*. Lund: Ethnologia Scandinavica.

Klepp, Ingun Grimstad. 2003b. *Fra rent til nyvasket. Skittent og rent tøy* [*From Clean to Newly Washed. Dirty and Clean Clothes*], No. 2. Nydalen: Statens Institutt for Forbruksforskning.

Klepp, Ingun Grimstad. 2004. "Farlige farger" ["Dangerous Colors"]. *Norsk antropologisk tidskrift* 15: 227–40.

Klepp, Ingun Grimstad. 2005. "The Meaning of Cleanliness: Modern Demonstrations of Female Purity." In Gro Gro Hagemann and Hege Roll-Hansen (eds) *Twentieth-century Housewives: Meanings and Implications of Unpaid Work*, pp. 191–216. Oslo: Unipub.

Klepp, Ingun Grimstad. 2006. *Skittentøyets kulturhistorie: hvorfor kvinner vasker klær* [*The Cultural History of Laundry: Why Women Wash Clothes*]. Oslo: Novus.

Larssen, Vetle Lid and Knut Bry. 2002. *Såpe: Kledd med Frelsesarmeen* [*Soap: Dressed with the Salvation Army*]. Oslo: Frelsesarmeen.

Latour, Bruno. 1998. *Artefaktens återkomst* [*The Return of the Artifact*]. Häftad: Nerenius & Santérus Förlag.

Lurie, Alison. 1981. *The Language of Clothes*. New York: Random House.

Maartmann, Camilla. 1998. *Kroppen som sjelens speil. En studie av den rene og kultiverte kroppen i mellomkrigstiden* [*The Body as the Mirror of the Soul. A Study of the Clean and Cultured Body in the Interwar Years*]. Oslo: Univeristetet i Oslo.

Martens, Lydia, Sue Scott and Matt Watson. 2003. "The Unbearable Lightness Of Cleaning": Representations of Domestic Practice and Products in *Good Housekeeping* Magazine (UK). Paper presented at the 2003 ESA Conference "Ageing Societies, New Sociology," The Consumption Network, September 23–26, Murcia, Spain.

Mauss, Marcel. 1979. *Sociology and Psychology: Essays*. London: Routledge & Kegan Paul.

Middleton, S., K. Ashworth and I. Braithwaite. 1997. *Small Fortune: Spending on Children, Childhood Poverty and Parental Sacrifice*. York: Joseph Rowntree Foundation.

Miller, Daniel. 1998. *A Theory of Shopping*. Cambridge: Polity Press.

Pettersen, Kristine. 2004. *Dress med Press: En studie av mannlig klesbruk i stortingssalen* [*Suits with Press: A Study of Male Dressing in the Norwegian Parliament*], No.

7. Nydalen: Statens Institutt for Forbruksforskning.

Rysst, Mari. 2006. "Barna kommer først: preferanser og utsatthet i norske barnefamilier" ["Children Come First: Preferences and Exposedness in Norwegian Families with Children"]. *Tidsskrift for Velferdsforskning* 2: 88–99.

Sandvik, Birte Cathrine. 1998. *Skikk og bruk, bruk og kast: Klesvaner i det moderne Norge* [*Manner and Etiquette, Consumerist Manners: Clothes Habits in Modern Norway*]. Oslo: B. C. Sandvik.

Schmidt, Lars Henrik and Jens Erik Kristensen (eds). 1986. *Lys, luft og renlighed: Den moderne socialhygiejnes fødsel* [*Light, Air and Cleanliness: The Birth of the Modern Social Hygiene*]. Copenhagen: Akademisk Forlag.

Schreier, Barbara A. 1989. "Sporting Wear." In Claudia Brush Kidwell and Valerie Steele (eds) *Men and Women: Dressing the Part*, pp. 92–123. Washington, DC: Smithsonian Institution Press.

Shove, Elizabeth. 2003a. *Comfort, Cleanliness + Convenience*. Oxford: Berg.

Solheim, Jorun 1998. *Den åpne kroppen: Om kjønnssymbolikk i moderne kultur* [*The Open Body: On Gender Symbolism in Modern Culture*]. Oslo: Pax.

SSB. 2002. Tidsbruksundersøkelsen 2000/2001 [Time Usage Survey]. Oslo: Statistisk sentralbyrå.

Statens Institutt for Forbruksforskning. 1977. *Barn og klede* [*Children and Clothes*]. Oslo: Statens Institutt for Forbruksforskning.

Steele, Valerie. 1989. *Men and Women: Dressing the Part*. Washington, DC: Smithsonian Institute.

Storm-Mathisen, Ardis and Ingun Grimstad Klepp. 2002. "People in Fashion—Adults of Style. The Impact of Fashion and Style on Clothing Choices: A Comparison of Accounts by Young Teenagers and Grown Women." *Fashion Theory* 9: 323–42.

Storm-Mathisen, Ardis and Ingun Grimstad Klepp. 2005. "Reading Fashion as Age: Teenage Girls and Grown Women's Accounts of Clothing as Body and Social Status." *Ethnologia Scandinavia* 36: 91–106.

Stoumann, Astrid. 1938. *With Dusting Cloth and Dustpan*, Copehagen: Gellerups forlag.

Sundt, Eilert. 1975. *Om Renligheds-Stellet i Norge: Til Oplysning om Flid og Fremskridt i Landet* [*On Cleanliness in Norway: To the Enlightenment on Diligence and Progress in the Country*]. Oslo: Gyldendal.

Torell, Viveka Berggren. 2003. *För Stass och Stoj: Barnkläder på 1900- talet utifrån mormors minnen och museers material* [*For Play and Festivity: Children's Clothes in the 20th Century Based on Grandma's Memories and the Material in Museums*]. Gothenburg: Etnologiska Föreningen i Västsverige.

Vigarello, Georges. 1998. *Concept of Cleanliness: Changing Attitudes in France since the Middle Aages*. Cambridge: Cambridge University Press.

Wilson, Elizabeth. 1985. *Adorned in Dreams: Fashion and Modernity* [*Kledd i draumar: Om mote*]. Oslo and London: Virago Press/Det Norske Samlaget.

Wintzell, Inga. 1972. *Så var barnen klädda: från kolt till täckjacka* [*How Children Were Dressed*]. Stockholm: Natur och kultur.

——. 1985. *Jeans och jeanskultur* [*Jeans and Jeans Culture*]. Stockholm: Nordiska museet.

Joseph Conrad's "The Planter of Malata": Timing, and the Forgotten Adventures of the Silk Plant "Arghan"

Joseph Conrad's 1914 short story "The Planter of Malata," set partly in Sydney and partly on the fictional island of "Malata," is a tale of unrequited passion ending with suicide (Conrad 1950). At the time the story is set, the planter Geoffrey Renouard is at a crucial juncture in his enterprise with something called silk plants. As I will establish, this particular short story of Conrad's is unusual in showing his political acuteness operating in a Pacific context, rather than in the English, Mediterranean European, Russian, or South American settings of his famously politically prescient fictions, and, furthermore, in a most unfamiliar field, that of economic botany.[1]

Written in the last two months of 1913, the story connects with the contemporary great race to discover an industrially viable artificial silk. And even more interesting is its prefiguring of a stock market scam of the early 1920s. Given the dates, Conrad could not possibly have known about the events surrounding the Arghan Company, which collapsed in 1924 with the loss of its £100,000 capital. Yet, as in Conrad's 1913 story, the 1919–24 Arghan story involved a kind of silk plant, potentially a very marketable and valuable fiber, being grown under conditions of some secrecy on a concession of land granted by a colonial government. So, as I show, the interest of Conrad's story is as a double narrative. One narrative is Conrad's to control, his story of finance and fashion, botany and romance. The other is history's narrative, which positions Conrad's story in the midst of a crucial period of innovations with vegetable and man-made silken fibers.

Conrad makes the planter Renouard's romantic crisis coincide with a critical middle stage of his long scientific work with silk plants. The opening scenes are set in Sydney. Renouard has brought his whole schooner full of the fiber from his plantation on Malata island, ready for transshipment to be sent on to Liverpool for experimental manufacture. While in Sydney, he is asked to dinner at the house of the retired eminent colonial statesman, old Dunster, who had been responsible for organizing the granting of the land concession on Malata to Renouard for his experimental work with silk plants. Amongst the guests at this dinner are three people traveling from England: Professor Moorsom, fashionable philosopher, touring lecturer, and author of bestselling books; his maiden sister; and his daughter, the stunning Felicia.

From this fateful occasion on, Renouard becomes increasingly enthralled by Felicia Moorsom, and diverted from his path of scientific endeavor into romance. The tale ends in tragedy. Renouard, "a man of action, and necessarily a believer in success" (p. 40), cannot win Miss Moorsom from her cold vanity of an idealized commitment to the object of her search, her missing fiancé. And, lacking the will to continue, he swims from Malata island out to sea beyond the point of return.

Most readers respond to the romantic human story, ignoring the realistic botanical story. With the focus on the human protagonists, "The Planter of Malata" is usually dismissed as a typical example of the weaknesses of Conrad's late-period romance writing. Taking up romance as a genre in order to appeal to the popular market of early-twentieth-century women readers, Conrad capitulates to, rather than commands, the mode he has chosen. The result of this artistic bad faith is slackly imagined scenes, pointless proliferation of unproductive imagery, and a narrative that simply reproduces Renouard's conventional sentimentality at passively extended length. For example:

> *He admired her voice as well poised as her movements, as her attitudes. He himself had always been a man of tranquil tones. But the power of fascination had torn him out of his very nature so completely that to preserve his habitual calmness from going to pieces had become a terrible effort.*

> *He used to go from her on board the schooner exhausted, broken, shaken up, as though he had been put to the most exquisite torture. When he saw her approaching he always had a moment of hallucination. She was a misty and fair creature, fitted for invisible music, for the shadows of love, for the murmurs of waters.*
> (pp. 34–5)

If, after persisting through this tiresome prose, we do care about Renouard, it is probably chiefly because Felicia, the darling of a society of froth and foam, fashion, fad, and fraud, is even worse than he is. The tragedy is less in Renouard's death than in the triumph of her shallow, fashionably sentimental ethos over his ethos of science, endeavor, and botanical innovation. At the end of Conrad's story Felicia leaves Malata with her father and aunt, sailing back to the metropolises of the lecture circuit, and eventually thence to the center of these circuits in social and economic London. However, Renouard's personal end, as he sets out "calmly to swim beyond the confines of life—with a steady stroke—his eyes fixed on a star!" is itself a good deal less poignant, it seems to me, than the fate of the mature silk plants in his abandoned plantation. Those plants, located "after five strenuous years of adventure and exploration," planted and successfully grown to maturity in the plantation on Malata, are pictured at the end of the story, a month or so after Renouard's death, as "growing rank and tall in the deserted fields." The story's key terms of fashion and finance are used in shaping the story of the human protagonists. As I show, these terms also apply to the overlooked non-human protagonists of the story, the silk plants.

"The Planter of Malata" is certainly not amongst Conrad's more commonly read works, and given the problems of the story as story, it is not surprising that the few longer discussions of it typically refer it to terms outside, autobiographical, psychological, or political. So, Conrad's difficulties with writing the name "Renouard" in his early manuscript of the tale may indicate that he associated himself with this character, cross-sexually, since "Renouard" resembles "Renouf," the name of the young woman Conrad unsuccessfully courted in Mauritius in 1888 while he was captaining a ship from Australia (Moser 1966). Or, alternatively, the story is psychologically interesting, if it can be read as Conrad's signal that he knows his art is tiring and realizes what sentimental direction it will take in future (Erdinast-Vulcan 1994: 187–200). Or, again, Conrad's falling into despair at his creative impasse is uncanny for the way it mirrors the political situation happening simultaneously in Europe. This was Edward Said's view in his first published book, *Joseph Conrad and the Fiction of Autobiography*: "With almost uncanny prescience his ability to harmonize past and present, action and thought, objective and subjective, failed him at just the moment that Europe's failed her" (Said 1966). Autobiographically, psychologically, or politically interesting—but what about scientifically?

Maybe the reason readers have not asked what the Planter of Malata's silk plants are is that they assume that the planter is growing mulberry trees. A close, literal reading of Conrad's story shows the identity of the silk plants to be actually a fascinatingly elusive mystery worth pursuing. What are these plants that they should be the subject of scientific, mercantile, financial, and political interest? What is Renouard's fiber? Attention to the details of this fiction reveals that mulberry trees are not at all the most likely silk plant candidate. That mulberries are not the plants in question is particularly evident in a remark of the story's splendidly disgusting Willie Dunster, nephew of the retired politician. This young Dunster is a "commercial monster" who runs an important Pacific trading office in Sydney. Renouard, who cannot stand the fellow, describes how he looks bat-like reading his correspondence, as he "holds the paper in both hands, hunches his shoulders up to his ugly ears, and brings his long nose and his thick lips to it like a sucking apparatus" (p. 4). He approves of Renouard's enterprise with the silk plants on anti-insectorial grounds: "Do away with the beastly cocoons all over the world" he buzzes, "in his blurred, waterlogged voice" (p. 33). So, clearly, whatever Renouard, "pioneer of the vegetable silk industry," is growing on Malata island, leased to him by the frugal colonial government, those plants are not fodder for silk worms. They are the raw material for a silk substitute.

What clues does the story give as to the identity of Renouard's silk plants? The catch-cry of "Planter," "the two big F's ... Fashion and Finance," would seem to have some application to "silk" plants. The would-be-witty coinage of this slogan is that of Renouard's friend and promoter, the editor and part-owner of the principle newspaper of this great colonial city, "the only literary newspaper in the Antipodes" (p. 14). "That's how I call it," he explains to Renouard. "There are three R's at the bottom of the social edifice and the two F's on the top ... And you proceed from one set to the other in this democratic age" (pp. 17–18). Various of the characters are drawn with clear reference to this slogan. The disgrace of the missing English fiancé of Felicia Moorsom that has driven him to exile in Australia then further exile on Malata island was a very ugly mess of a financial character, something of a criminal order. Since his departure from England, however, new evidence has emerged that clears him of the crime, but he cannot be located to be told. Felicia now determines, out of strong-willed and fashionably noble impulse, to pursue him, and marry him. She is perfectly capable of doing this, being of age and with money of her own, and plenty of determination. But since she is the professor's only surviving child, and a brilliant London socialite, she "isn't the kind of everyday young lady who may be permitted to gallop around the world all by herself," and the father has had to respond to the unwelcome exigency philosophically. He has evidently concluded it would be "more truly paternal, more prudent too, and generally safer all round to let himself be dragged into this chase." The aunt has come along for the same reason, to save public face, and to make it appear this is "a trip round the world of the usual kind."

Again, under the same aegis of the "F & F" slogan, Professor Moorsom's success is that he is the "fashionable philosopher of the age," with material interests as well as philosophical, and with an eye to a good investment, for example, Renouard's silk plant enterprise on Malata.

Professor Moorsom's sister is another instance of Fashion. That "maiden lady in her wonderful preservation," who reminds Renouard "somehow of a wax flower under glass," dresses very well, in expensive gowns becoming her age, and she also judges Renouard by his clothing:

She did not like him very much in the afternoons, in his white drill suit and planter's hat, which seemed to her an unduly Bohemian costume for calling in a house where there were ladies. But in the evening, lithe and elegant in his dress clothes and with his pleasant, slightly veiled voice, he always made her conquest afresh. He might have been anybody distinguished—the son of a duke! (p. 44)

As for Felicia herself, she is the "fashionable and clever beauty," "London hostess to tip-top people ever since she put her hair up." That "great wealth of hair," burnished red-coppery gold, together with the jet-black of her eyes and the marble of her complexion and ivory of her skin, combine to enthrall Renouard. To him, she appears a being "made of ivory and precious metals changed into living tissue," an alchemical Coppelia.

Given the story's commitment to the "Fashion and Finance" idea, the most readily envisaged use for Renouard's vegetable silk is cloth for clothing, esteemed as the highest use to which a fiber may be put, though comparatively few fibers are suitable (Dodge 1897: 27). The market for silk itself in the late nineteenth century had been significantly expanded in England by the fashion set by Queen Victoria for extended mourning. The material most associated with mourning was black silk crepe, and, for jewelry, jet. Showing contempt for this fashion of the dead, Conrad really has it in for his character Felicia Moorsom, of the jet eyes, who, though not really a widow, is quite ready to throw herself into a prolonged period of mourning for the missing ex-fiancé, Arthur, who is a good deal more attractive to her in his absence.

Silk's high value as a clothing material is because of its luster, its fineness, its strength in proportion to its light weight, its elasticity, its power to absorb moisture, its affinity for dye, and its warmth, since it is a poor conductor of heat. Several of these qualities also made silk the best choice for a diverse range of other products—from stockings to wallpaper, for early airplanes and parachutes, and even for use in experimental knee surgery from as early as 1903. In that year, F. Lange of Munich performed the first anterior cruciate ligament replacement, using braided silk to replace the ligament. This fact would have interested Conrad intimately, if he had known about it, since his wife had to have surgery for exactly this crippling ligament problem, a disability that had a profound and long-term effect on the family. However, with the same quirks of timing that characterize the whole relation between Conrad's story of the silk substitute and developments in this area of textile history, Lange's groundbreaking ligament replacement surgery was a year before Jessie Conrad's operation, and was not more successful than hers, though the idea of using silk to replace the ligament did lead in the right direction for future successful surgical developments.[2]

Silk, however, was expensive, sensitively so around the time Conrad was forming his ideas for this story. For, while England—the country Conrad elected to make his permanent home from 1886—was encouraging free trade policies, the United States was assisting its fledgling silk industry by protectionism. This protectionism took the form of extraordinarily high tariffs on superior European silk fabric imports. From 1864, the American tariff on European silk goods was raised to 60%, while raw silk from Asia, ready for American power loom weaving, was admitted free of duty in 1865 (Furuta 2005: 211). Encouraged by the more favorable conditions in the United States, artisans from England and France naturally chose to emigrate.

Political reasons aside, silk was anyway an expensive fabric.

Some 2,500 cocoons are needed to make one yard (that is, just under a meter) of silk fabric. The processes of winding the silk filaments off cocoons to form a hank of silk thread (silk reeling) and twisting of one or more silk threads together to form a much stronger thread (silk throwing) involve time and skill, especially on the part of the throwster (Zanier 2005: 113). As far back as 1664, the English naturalist Robert Hooke had theorized that it might be possible to spin an artificial filament out of a substance like that which silk worms secrete, and over the years many scientists tried to produce an artificial silk.

The first success was nearly 200 years later. In 1855, the Frenchman George Audemars was able to make a thread by dipping a needle into a viscous solution of mulberry bark pulp and rubber. But his process was very slow, and required a great deal of skill and precision. The first economically viable synthetic silk fiber was produced and patented in 1884 by Count Hilaire Chardonnet in France after twenty-nine years of research. A drawback was that his pretty fabric, known as "Chardonnet silk," was also very flammable. But the race was definitely on. Another patenter of an artificial silk, famous not for his silk inventions but rather for his success with explosive material of a different kind, was Alfred Nobel, inventor of dynamite. Finally, in 1891–2, the English chemists Charles Cross and Edward Bevan invented a safe process for turning plant fiber, cellulose, into a viscous state suitable for spinning. Manufacturers found this "viscose" process viable, and Courtaulds Fibres, which had earlier been the main producer of silk crepe, produced the first viscose rayon in 1905 (Coleman 1969).[3]

By the mid-1920s, textile manufacturers in the United States could buy rayon for half the price of raw silk. And, meanwhile, other experiments with cellulose led to the invention of other different kinds of artificial silk. Taking off in a different direction, another successful process was the acetate process. Acetate was developed into celluloid film for motion pictures, and it was used for dope, a type of lacquer for protecting, waterproofing, and tautening cloth surfaces on airplane wings during the First World War.[4]

So Conrad's story is contemporaneous with great developments in artificial silks. However, the name of "artificial silk" for these man-made fibers is in one important way misleading, because, although they resemble silk in luster and general appearance, in tensile strength artificial silk has about one-half the breaking strain of natural silk, and its elasticity is also about one-third to one-half of natural silk (Merritt Matthews 1916: 352, 375–6). Therefore, simultaneous with the race to develop imitation silks was a great race to find a natural fiber with silk's strength, that was capable of being spun fine enough that it could be employed in the manufacture of cloth or woven fabric (Dodge 1897: 27–8).

Conrad's Renouard has managed, as the reward of his strenuous "five years' programme of scientific adventure, of work, of danger and endurance" to locate and transfer, then successfully plant and raise on his Malata plantation in quantity to maturity a kind of silk plant that has "eminent capitalists at home...very much interested." At the time his path disastrously crosses with the fashionable Moorsom crowd, he is, after an interval of waiting for the shipment to reach Liverpool and be tested, about to discover whether or not the fiber he has produced will meet the high standards required to appeal to manufacturers. And even if the experimental manufacture of thread and cloth produces a desirable item, his fiber plant will still have to chance its luck in finding a manufacturer willing to back it financially, who already has or will develop the machinery needed to manufacture it, and who succeeds in finding a market. Renouard's affairs are indeed at a critical and crucially uncertain juncture. It is easier for the Dunster-type politicians and businessmen confidently to envisage the future: once Renouard meets with mercantile success his "next public task," so the old politician Dunster tells him, will be to make "a careful survey of the Northern Districts to discover tracts suitable for the cultivation of the silk plant." And young Dunster, the Cobden Club economist, foresees far-reaching effects for Renouard's plants, providing he succeeds: "You may yet change the history of our country. For economic conditions do shape the history of nations."

It is odd that this story was not and is not discussed in terms of its political and botanical topicality. Conrad himself thought its original form too riskily close to reality, and the alterations he made to his manuscript to obscure some references show him tempering his risk-taking impulse with more prudent reconsiderations. He anticipated trouble if readers thought they could identify originals for the characters in his story, and its Australian location. Therefore, in his manuscript he removed the specification of Sydney as the "great colonial city," and when the story was in proofs he made a further change he regarded as being of great urgency. He wrote to his agent J. B. Pinker in January 1914, "I have a further request to make—very important and that is that the name Deacon throughout the story should be replaced by the name Dunster. There is good reason for this." Conrad's "good reason" was probably that Deacon (which Conrad had spelt as with the church minister) is a homonym of the Australian Prime Minister Deakin, "well-known in Britain for his role in winning Parliament's assent to Australian federation" (Karl and Davies 1996: 329).[5] Eight years after Australian Federation in 1901, Deakin became the leader of the new Fusion Party, the merger of free trade and protectionist anti-socialists, and in 1910 these free-traders and Deakinites began calling themselves the Liberal Party, ancestor of the present-day party. So the subject of Cobdenite Free Trade principles in an Australian context was topical at the time Conrad was writing his story, with its Cobdenite economist character, Young Dunster. The same subject had been even more contentious earlier, at the time of his five voyages to Australia as a seaman between 1879 and 1893. Since Conrad spent a total of about seventeen months in Australian ports during this time, he had plenty of opportunity to witness the arguments about free trade that raged through the pre-Federation 1870s and 1880s, divided the Australian press, the political parties, and the Australian colonies. Together with continuing jealousies and rivalries amongst the six colonies, the disagreements about whether to opt for free trade or for protectionist policies delayed significant progress towards Federation until the 1890s.[6]

Conrad anticipated a more inquisitive reading, and a more politically knowing reception of his story than it received. The Sydney *Bulletin* newspaper, producing its literary "Red Page" during the same period of 1880s and 1890s when Conrad was at various times in Sydney as seaman, was a probable model for the description of the newspaper in Conrad's story. The Sydney *Bulletin* would be, to Conrad's English-speaking readership (Conrad's early books were also published in separate editions "for distribution in British colonies and dependencies only"), a good candidate for identification as "the only literary newspaper in the Antipodes." And the same Sydney *Bulletin*, when it reviewed Conrad's story in 1915, is the place where you would most expect any topical Australian political and economic-botanical issues to be discussed.[7] That did not happen, though the reviewer did identify the city as Sydney, and the newspaper as his own. He was chiefly struck by Conrad's scene in the editorial room where they have "been feasting a poet from the bush, the latest discovery of the Editor." As Conrad says of his character, and as, with permissible exaggeration, could equally be said of the *Bulletin*'s real owner-editor, J. F. Archibald, during the years Conrad was occasionally in Australia, "Such discoveries [as the poet from the bush] were the business, the vocation, the pride and delight of the only apostle of letters in the hemisphere, the solitary patron of culture, the Slave of the Lamp—as he subscribed himself at the bottom of the weekly literary page of his paper." The *Bulletin*'s reviewer of Conrad's story reacts with mock incredulity to this scene in the editorial room where the poet whom the editor has been entertaining, too generously it seems, has fallen asleep on the office hearth-rug. "Do editors really do such things in Sydney?" he asks. But, though he does invite readers to identify the Sydney character in a different one of Conrad's stories in the same volume, the Frenchman without hands (they have been blown off when he was fishing using dynamite) whom Conrad has as a tobacco seller at the lower end of Sydney city's George Street, the 1915 *Bulletin* reviewer is not interested in who either of the Dunsters might be, or in silk plants.

The identity of anything called a "silk plant" is not easy to determine. "Silk plant" is not a generic name: a range of different plants are called silk plants or silk grass because of their lustrous appearance, and many of these can be excluded as candidates for Renouard's plantation. This is true of the plant popularly known as "vegetable silk" or, alternatively, "cotton grass." Though the fiber presents a beautiful silky appearance it is entirely unsuited for the manufacture of textiles, so Renouard, "pioneer of the vegetable silk industry," is most unlikely to be growing the plant actually named "vegetable silk" (Merritt Matthews 1916: 347).

Supposing Conrad had a particular plant in mind, the description of the mature Malata plantation's appearance helps to identify possible candidates. A scene that is presented after Renouard, desperately hoping not to lose Miss Moorsom, has brought all three Moorsoms to Malata in search of the missing ex-fiancé Arthur, shows Professor Moorsom's white parasol "bobbing up here and there like a buoy adrift on a sea of dark green plants." The human figure in the plantation brings together the theme of fashion and clothing and the theme of economic botany. As the professor, fashionably attired and with cloth umbrella, scrutinizes the plantation with a view to investment, his figure lends proportion to the size of the plantation field, and also gives an idea of the height, color, and density of the mature plants. One first-rate fiber plant that fits this description had been attracting a good deal of well-established competitive international attention and investment by the time Conrad was writing his story. China grass or white ramie, *Boehmeria nivea*, is a shrubby plant with the habit of a common nettle, but without the stinging hairs. At the time the plant is ready for harvesting there are numerous straight shoots that rise out of the perennial rootstock to a height of 5–7 feet. There is also a more robust variant form, known as green ramie, Indian ramie, or rhea. Fiber produced from both forms is valued because of its strength and durability: of all fibers tested at the turn of the century it was the least affected by moisture. Furthermore, its filaments can be separated almost to the fineness of silk, and it can be dyed successfully, sometimes with results as lustrous and brilliant as silk. French interest in ramie dated from the 1830s, when ramie seed was first introduced into France, and, illustrating the way in which the history of ships and seamen ties in with the history of plants, in 1844 plants brought from China by the surgeon of a French warship were being grown in the acclimatizing gardens. By 1850, the plant was being cultivated in the botanical gardens in Munich, and in 1860 in Belgium. It was introduced into the United States in 1855, though not in fact successfully grown until 1867, further south, in Mexico (Dodge 1897: 91). After it was established that the plant could be grown outside its native Eastern habitats (Assam, China, Japan, and the Malay Archipelago), the next challenge was to invent machines that would make manufacture affordable. In China and Japan the fiber was extracted by hand labor, not a financial proposition for production in Europe or the United States. In a story that is worth recalling for its typicality of the kinds of problems faced by any new promising economic fiber plant, the Government of India in 1869 offered a reward of £5,000 for the best machine to decorticate the green stalks. The first exhibition and trial of 1872 produced no successes, nor did the ten machines exhibited at a further official trial in 1879. Though the immediate result was to stimulate invention in many countries, much money being outlaid in the process and much lost along the way, the problem of machinery remained recalcitrant (Dodge 1897: 85–7; Goulding 1917: 124–9). In 1916, an American authority on textile fibers was still noting that "the chief difficulty in the way of [Ramie's] universal and widespread adoption has been the lack of an efficient process for properly decorticating the fibre from the rest of the plant" (Merritt Matthews 1916: 412). So, if ramie is what Conrad's Renouard is cultivating, his success is very far from assured, as Conrad may very well have been thinking when he situated his story at this juncture of Renouard's work. As with the uncertain and maybe tragic future of ventured romance, so with the uncertain future of venture planting.

The case of ramie shows how attuned Conrad's story is to contemporary events, in this case events of economic botany it was possible he could have known about. The case of a different "silk plant," Arghan (also known by its Spanish name pita) demonstrates, even in a slimly imagined short story such as this, Conrad's instinct for a fertile issue. Finance also figured largely in the disastrous future adventures of this mystery silk plant whose fiber promised to be a better alternative for British manufacturers than other superior fibers, including cotton, flax, and various hemps in high demand, which had to be bought on markets not under British control. Preliminary tests on Arghan had shown it to have remarkable salt-water-resisting power, and strength, and it was predicted that British manufacturers would gladly use it for their finest products in preference to comparable fibers already on the market. And, furthermore, it could be grown in British colonies and dependencies (Figure 1).[8]

The Arghan Company, under the chairmanship of Abraham Montefiore, a German-Jewish financier, was incorporated in London in November 1919 with an initial capital of £40,000, at a time when—to give a sense of proportion to that figure—a white-collar worker's annual salary was about £200. The company's advisor was Henry Wickham, a great asset to them as the "highly reputable pioneer" of the British rubber plantation industry. He received a knighthood in 1920 for his services to the rubber industry. More than forty years earlier, in 1876, Wickham had taken 70,000 *Hevea braziliensis* rubber tree seeds from Amazonia and delivered them to Dr Joseph Hooker at the Royal Botanical Gardens at Kew (Wickham 1908; Lane 1953, 1953–4).[9] The *Hevea* seedlings propagated at Kew were subsequently dispatched to various parts of the British Empire, including Ceylon, Singapore, and Malaya, and their eventually successful growth in British territories led to the breaking of the monopoly on wild rubber on the external market. In this way, the history of rubber repeated, with comparably enormous

Figure 1
Bromeliaceae *Bromelia magdalenae* (Andre) C. H. Wright; artifact description: pita fiber; geography description: Colombia; common name: pita; part held: leaves; Kew Centre for Economic Botany catalog number: 29706; date 1920.

influential results for Britain, the earlier pattern with cinchona, the Amazonian tree whose bark produces quinine, which, following initiatives from Kew, had finally been successfully transplanted in British India in the early 1860s (Brockway 1979: 117–21).

Henry Wickham [1846–1928] had begun his career as a pioneer planter and adventurer in the same South American Orinoco and Amazon River areas as the earlier famous British botanical explorers, cinchona collector Richard Spruce and his friend Alfred Russel Wallace, later the great ethnographer of the Malay Archipelago, who had traveled with Spruce in the Amazon basin in 1848–52 (Spruce 1908). Wickham was a latter-day imperial patriot who, though without any such botanical training as Spruce, sought throughout his life to be of service to his country by locating useful new plants that could be transferred within the Empire, repeatedly recommending what he regarded as the best way of planting, harvesting, and treating them, and inventing new machines for processing. In the latter endeavors he was never successful, and in the former only successful with the *Hevea* transfer, for which he was finally knighted in 1920. Wickham had become interested in the plant later called "Arghan" in the late 1880s, during his time in British Honduras, where the plant was known as "silk grass." Nothing followed at that stage, but twenty-five years later, with problems in Russian flax supply causing a 70% annual world shortage of that fiber, with American cotton supplies increasingly taken up by American manufacturers, and with alternative fine fibers costly, a plant with Arghan's promising manufacturing test results, which could be grown in territories where

Figure 2
Bromeliaceae *Bromelia magdalenae* (Andre) C. H. Wright; artifact description: silk grass fiber; geography: Belize (British Honduras); common name: silk grass?; part held: leaves; Kew catalog number: 29704; date 1923.

land and labor were under British control looked a very attractive investment (Figure 2).[10]

Following incorporation as a stock market company, the Arghan Company advised by Wickham sent an expedition to British Honduras, its purpose, as Montefiore said, "to investigate and obtain supplies of Arghan plants from their native habitats in the wilds with the object of transplanting these into organized areas of British dominions in the East on lines similar to those which proved so successful in the rubber industry." After fifteen months of labor, the plants were transported to the Federated Malay States. At the Extraordinary General Meeting of April 1922, Montefiore reported that he had secured for the company a valuable concession of 30,000 acres in any part of the Federated Malay States, free from all premium, with the nominal land rent starting at fifty cents per acre per annum, rising to a maximum of one dollar per acre per annum, as against a substantial premium of four dollars per acre per annum that rubber estates were paying. And there were plans for further plantations in India and Ceylon. Montefiore also reported at this extraordinary general meeting, whose purpose was to increase the capital of the company from £40,000 in 400,000 two-shilling shares to £100,000 in 1,000,000 two-shilling shares, that the Government of Ceylon was prepared to grant a concession of 30,000 acres, and that no less a figure than the Secretary of State for the Colonies, Mr Winston Churchill, had communicated his support for the company by telegraph to the Governor of Ceylon.[11]

At this time in early 1922 the company was reporting very favorable progress with growing the plants and getting the approval of cloth manufacturers. The chairman reported to the shareholders that the company now had a nursery of sixty acres of flourishing plants, and had succeeded in spinning the fiber to 7,500 yards per pound (lb), with results which showed that it could be spun to a very much finer count. Results had also been achieved in dyeing, weaving, and the manufacture of various cloths that had won the enthusiastic appreciation of the master textile experts in Belfast, Dundee, and Lancashire. To maximize efficiency, the plants distributed from the company nursery were going to be grown by subsidiary companies on plantations of 5,000 acres each. It was intended that the Arghan Company would in each case receive a substantial consideration for the transfer of its land grants, the plants supplied, and the expert advice offered. In October the chairman drew attention to the fact that the current price of two fine fibers, cotton and flax were currently £130 and £180 per ton. Arghan, he said, was superior to both of these fibers, and could be produced at considerably less than half the cost of either. Montefiore also said that the Arghan Company had made excellent progress in getting so far at so modest expense in only three years, and that the late Mr Joseph Chamberlain, the ex-Prime Minister, had lost nearly £100,000 in endeavoring to establish sisal in the West Indies.[12] This was an odd and in hindsight ominous way to make the point that Arghan's progress was unusually fast and inexpensive.

In 1922 there was no public intimation of any uncertainty about Arghan's future. The scientific and manufacturing tests commissioned on the fiber found it to be exceptional. The Managing Director the Belfast Ropework Company reported that:

I have carried out exhaustive and reliable tests on the samples of your fibre submitted to me, and I am thoroughly satisfied from the results obtained that Arghan is a fibre of a very high order, and which should prove an asset of the greatest commercial value in the textile world, as it is capable of being extensively used in the production of goods of the highest quality.

Although your fibre is much too good for most of the classes of articles produced by the Belfast Ropework Co., Ltd., and other firms in the same branch of the trade, I feel sure that they will gladly use it for their finest products in preference to either Manilla, Italian, Russian or Indian hemps.

Its salt-water-resisting qualities are remarkable and its tensile strength is abnormal, giving a breaking strain of more than 50 per cent over that

Figure 3
Bromeliaceae *Bromelia magdalenae* (Andre) C. H. Wright; artifact description: Arghan fiber; geography: Singapore, Grove Estate, Malesia; common name: Arghan; part held: leaves; Kew catalog number: 29705; date 1924.

obtained in the same class of goods manufactured from the finest Italian hemp or the best flax.

At the same Extraordinary General Meeting where Montefiore read out the Belfast Ropework Company's assessment he also read a report by Messrs. Cross and Bevan, the analysts to the Federated Malay States Government. These two scientists, who Montefiore said "are, I think, regarded as the top of the tree of analysts in this country," were the same Charles Cross and Edward Bevan who were the discoverers and patenters of the two great new processes for making artificial fibre—the viscose process (1892) and the cellulose acetate process (1894). Their report shows clearly and with detailed precision why the excitement over Arghan was justified. Even with the strands untwisted the fiber was found to be exceptionally strong:

Gentlemen, at the request of the Federated Malay States Government we have submitted your fibre to full investigation, and we may at once say that of the innumerable fibres submitted to us during our long professional practice, of potential industrial importance, Arghan stands out pre-eminent.

The structural qualities of the strands are remarkable, the breaking strain, determined on silk-testing machines, gives numbers for weight/length unit superior to those of the staple textile fibres of all classes. Those who have technical experience will find this statement justified by the following figures, noting that the tests were made on the untwisted strands of the original fibre.

We find a range of 3.0 to 6.1 grammes per 1 denier, for breaking strain; and extensibility—1.8 to 2.5 per cent. The "tenacity" figures are quite remarkable, and they establish the Arghan fibre and fibre substance as a new and exceptional type.

Messrs Cross and Bevan anticipated that the fiber would be further improved once a suitable method of industrial preparation was selected, but judging it even in its present state of preparation they were confident of a preeminent manufacturing future:

The fibre should take premier place as a staple for fine twine, lines and cordages, and, from the sample of cloth which you have submitted to us, its textile possibilities are shown to be very considerable.

On one further crucial count Arghan fiber was demonstrably superior, in its salt-water resistance:

Sea Water Immersion Tests—We subjected a sample of the original fibre in the free state to a month's immersion in the ocean tank at the Biological Station, Plymouth, and it is satisfactory to note that the degree of chemical resistance of the fibre was of a very high order. In the same circumstances cotton, flax, etc., would have been degraded in composition and entirely disintegrated as regards structure. On the result of our investigations, which have been prolonged, we have formed a strong view of the importance of your fibre as a technical discovery of great industrial importance.

In his diary Sir Henry Wickham kept a copy of the Arghan Company Report of the Extraordinary General Meeting in which these test results were published, along with newspaper cuttings from French and English newspapers reporting Arghan developments. But he was not destined to make money out of his "discovery."

The Arghan enterprise all came to nothing. The promised concession of 30,000 acres in a location anywhere the company liked to choose in the Federated Malay States, as announced by Montefiore in the Extraordinary General Meeting in April 1922, did not eventuate, and by October the Arghan Company had to settle for a different arrangement, whereby rubber plantation companies would cooperate in planting the young Arghan plants, each company receiving sufficient plants for ten acres, free. But the plants were not thriving in their new Malayan location. The 1922 Annual Report of the Chief Secretary of the Federated Malay States stated:

The Company has been unfortunate. It was given land at Rompin (Pahang) and surrendered it as the land was unsuitable. It was then given land near Teluk Anson, and has recently been compelled to surrender it also, for the same

Figure 4
Bromeliaceae *Bromelia magdalenae* (Andre) C. H. Wright; artifact description: pita string and fiber; geography: Colombia; common name: pita; part held: leaves; Kew catalog number: 29701; date 1929.

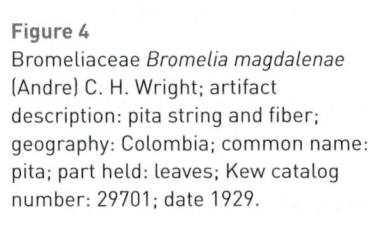

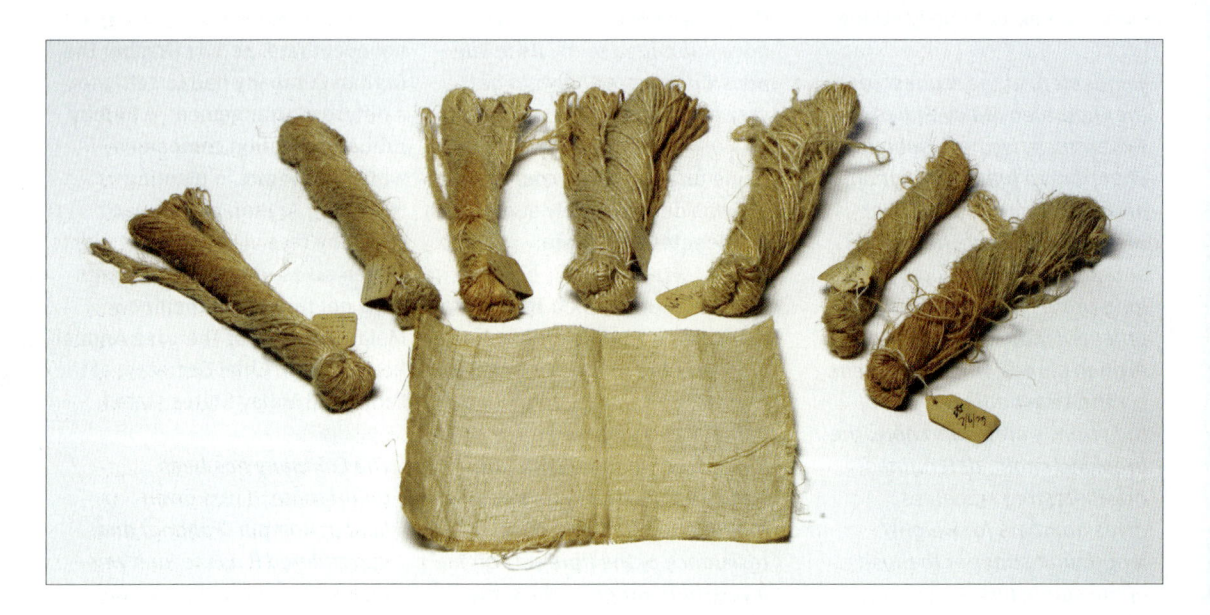

Figure 5
Bromeliaceae *Bromelia magdalenae* (Andre) C. H. Wright; artifact description: pita fiber and yarn; geography: Colombia; common name: pita; part held: leaves; Kew catalog number: 29707; date 1929.

reason. The Company is now seeking land elsewhere. There are less than 7,000 plants in the country, and they are small and immature. The nurseries in which they are kept cover only half an acre (cited in Lane January 23, 1954: 9).

The shortage of plants was such a serious problem that in January 1923 one of the company's directors, S. Douglas Harding, together with a horticulturalist, John Russell, went back to British Honduras to collect 25,000 suckers and several ounces of silk grass seed. But by this time it was too late to save the company, which was wound up in September 1924, with all of the capital gone. Montefiore himself died the same year.[13]

However, even if the plants had thrived, the problem of decortication may have ended the Arghan Company. Despite prolonged efforts, no fully successful machine has ever been developed that can satisfactorily decorticate the leaves of this plant. Furthermore, competing American companies had proven that, far from being a plant "discovered and pioneered" by Henry Wickham, and far from being growable only in British territories, the plant newly named "Arghan" was in fact a South American plant whose fiber had been known and sold in Europe since at least the 1800s (Ticktin 2002: 92).

"Arghan" was actually the bromeliad *Aechmea magdalenae*, named by the French botanist Edouard François André in 1888 (as *Chevaliera magdalenae*) after the Magdalene River, a tributary of the Orinoco, where he had found the plant during his arduous botanical collecting trip of 1875–6. *Aechmea magdalenae* is an enormous member of the pineapple family. It has leaves of up to 2.5 m (ten feet or more) in length, and it grows along streams, in swampy areas, and on hillsides in lowland neotropical rainforests from Mexico to Ecuador. Spectacular in appearance, and extraordinary for its properties as a fiber, *Aechmea magdalenae* is also remarkable for the way it sometimes grows in large monospecific clusters, which so resemble plantations that they were called "pitales," plantation-like but not planted, an anachronistic marvel of old nature imitating European civilization's proud horticultural art of plantations (Bunting 1924; Dawe cited in *Bulletin of the Imperial Institute* 1920; Stockdale 1923).[14]

For centuries before it possessed its botanic name, *Aechmea magdalenae* was highly regarded for its exceptional properties as a fiber. Probably domesticated in the pre-Columbian period, it was known in South America as ixtle or pita,[15] and the long white fiber extracted from its giant spiny leaves was valued for its strength and durability, and resistance to salt water. In Mexico, indigenous peoples used ixtle in a multiplicity of ways. The fiber was used for rope, fishing nets and lines, bags, fans, sandals, sewing thread and strings for musical instruments, especially the *jaranas* of Veracruz. The leaf once the fiber was removed was braided into hammocks, the thorns of ixtle leaves were employed as needles, while the juice of the leaves was used as a caustic for wounds. The pineapple-like fruit was edible.[16] Because of its qualities as a saltwater-resistant fiber for ropes, ixtle was later used as rigging for sailing ships crossing the Atlantic. And in the Spanish colonial period and into the nineteenth century, "Colombian pita" or "silk grass" as it was known in Europe, was being extracted in quantity and exported to Europe, especially from Colombia and British Honduras (Ticktin 2002: 92)—the same British Honduras where Henry Wickham would later claim to have "discovered and pioneered" it.

The history of bromeliads in Europe dates back to Christopher Columbus's second voyage to the New World for Queen Isabella of Spain in 1493. Struck with the find of such a splendidly bizarre-looking and exotically tasty fruit, he brought the pineapple, still the most famous member of the bromeliad family, back home with him from the West Indies, and it was later cultivated in the Old World tropics. By 1549 it was successfully grown in India. When the first pineapple was grown in England it was presented to King Charles II by his gardener, and the episode was so momentous that it was recorded in a portrait now hanging in the Victoria and Albert Museum in London (Benzing 1980: 1).

In the late nineteenth century, Europe, scientifically more intercooperative than in the years to follow, began to take keen interest in other members of the pineapple family, for other reasons than taste and exotic appearance. Charles Edouard Morren, born in Belgium in

1833, had become the recognized authority on Bromeliaceae by the 1870s. He collected bromeliads in the Botanic Gardens at Liège, where he was director. Many of the very high-quality drawings he made of these plants may be seen at the Royal Botanic Gardens at Kew.[17] The namer of *Aechmea magdalenae*, Edouard François André, was a student of Morren. On his collecting trips in Colombia and Ecuador in 1875–76 André carried with him letters of introduction from English fellow botanist Richard Spruce (1908).[18] After returning to France, André studied his collections carefully over many years and eventually in 1889 published a great monograph entitled *Bromeliaceae Andreanae*, a detailed account of the 122 species and fourteen varieties he had collected in South America. Ninety-one of these were new to science. A gifted German scientist, Carl Mez was another of Morren's students. His long and exceptionally thorough study led to his 1934–5 publication, in Adolf Engler's *Das Pflanzenreich*, of the most extensive monograph on the Bromeliaceae to date. He also conducted a brilliant series of experiments to discover how the hair-like trichomes on a bromeliad's leaves absorb salts and moisture (Benzing 1980: 3). However, the advent of the First World War diverted enthusiasm away from horticultural research generally, though it was rumored that fiber from *Aechmea magdalenae* was being used in the construction of German aircraft wings. During the wartime years many collections of living and preserved plants were devastated, and even greater destruction occurred in the Second World War, with the loss of more greenhouse collections and herbaria. Since 1945, interest in bromeliads has risen again, this time not only in Europe but also in the USA, Australia, New Zealand, and elsewhere, though mainly because of the desirability of some of the exquisite varieties for gardens. Back in its native Mexico and Northern Guatemala, *Aechmea magdalenae* has settled to a very different, and much more limited, career of usefulness than was once, in the starry days of Arghan, predicted for it. Today, ixtle, as *Aechmea magdalenae* is popularly called in Mexico, is valued for its silvery thread used to embroider leather articles such as belts, saddles, and sombreros in a popular and expensive kind of artwork known as *el piteado*. The main consumers of *piteado* products are the cowboy culture of Mexico and the Southern United States; police officers in some Northern States of Mexico where the embroidered belt is part of the uniform; and Mexican drug traffickers, for whom the expensive items, particularly the saddles, are a sign of status. Much of the recent production of *piteado* products has been carried out by prisoners as an activity promoted in jails in Sonora and Baja California (Ticktin 2002: 93–4).

This plant had such a noble working past as pita domestically, and intercontinentally in colonial times. It entered European botanical classification as *Aechmea* (or *Bromelia*) *magdalenae* in the late nineteenth century, but its fiber was not commonly distinguished from that of a variety of other pita plants. In view of its disastrous second European transit as an economic plant, an important question is—was its 1920s incarnation as Arghan a morally shady episode in the global biography of this plant? Presented mysteriously to the public as Arghan, this plant would appear to be a product and a casualty of the same Fashionable world of London botanical stock market Finance that Conrad touched on in his short story about another silk plant in another colonial concession. By the loss of shareholders' money in the sudden 1924 collapse of the Arghan Company, and by the apparent secrecy of the new naming of the plant, it might seem that some deception was involved.

Given Henry Wickham's often-expressed disapproval of Britain's sharing of information about economic plants and their manufacture with foreign countries, there may have been a xenophobic motive in newly naming the plant. Perhaps it was hoped that, by keeping the familiar identity of the plant secret,[19] a stance would be made against this anti-Imperialistic openness, which Wickham inveighed against in his 1908 book *On the Plantation, Cultivation, and Curing of Para Indian Rubber* as "the usual course of liberality and open-handed way of our Government authorities, after first having taken the initiative and cost, they have been passed on to other than our own equatorial possessions and colonies—widely—to those of German, French, Dutch, in Africa, Oceana, Java, and Borneo, etc., throughout the equatorial belt" (quoted in Lane January 30, 1954: 5).

But was there financial deception? The credibility of Abraham Montefiore (previously Abraham Rosenthal who had changed his name to take his wife's), was much questioned in the correspondence of the various British Malay government officials and botanical advisors discussing the company's applications for land.[20] They were also suspicious of the company's refusal to identify the fiber plant. In short, was the venture speculative or actually honest? Was Montefiore himself an "untruthful Jew," "a slippery Jew," attempting a gigantic stock-selling swindle? Was the Arghan Company merely a promoting company that wanted "to get hold of a large concession which they can hawk round for sale"? And what relation if any, was the Arghan Company to Eastern Cultivation Ltd, operating from the same Pinners Hall address in London, but making separate bids for land in Malaya to cultivate Arghan?

Though the Arghan venture was mismanaged financially and botanically, probably there was no deception. Montefiore himself was evidently a confirmed believer in Wickham, and in 1920 he had also become chairman of the new Roa Company, to exploit the "Roa" rubber smoke curing machine designed by Robert Legg in collaboration with Wickham (Lane January 30, 1954: 6). The Arghan Company was aiming to distinguish itself by making much faster progress than was usual with plantation and manufacturing ventures, and at a much more modest cost. In 1922, £100,000 capital is equivalent to approximately £3.6 million in 2005 using the UK Retail Prices Index as an adjustment factor. This is far too small a sum to float a company in today's financial markets and, on the face of it, the Arghan Company would appear to have been undercapitalized from the outset. Montefiore mentioned that as regards Ceylon, the Government of the Colony had estimated it would cost between one million and one and a quarter million pounds to develop the 30,000 acres concession there. So, the Arghan Company, capitalized from 1922 at £100,000 was probably altogether too idealistic and optimistic, though optimism certainly seems to have been warranted by the outstanding results of the scientific tests on Arghan fiber.

The disastrous fate of the Arghan venture in Malaya was spectacular and extreme compared with than that of Renouard and his silk plants in Malata. By the time of the company's collapse in 1924, the Arghan plants in the field were not growing wild and rank—they were all dead. The newly imported plants were sold off to various other Malayan plantations. In Conrad's story, before Renouard ends his own life he has the humanity to order that all his workers be paid off with cash, and be returned by the visiting trading vessel to their respective homes. By contrast, the European manager and his assistants on the Arghan estate in Malaya had been left for months without their salaries, living as best they could, and the whole of the Chinese labor force had to be taken off by the local authorities and fed from the police station in Kuala Lipis.[21]

Joseph Conrad, who knew by painful first-hand experience the dangers of optimistic financial venturing (Najder 1983: 71, 89, 92, especially 201), has all the main characters in "The Planter of Malata" acting through motives and making choices that are at one and the same time idealistic and also rather morally dubious though innocently so. This especially includes Renouard, whose first decision not to talk about his unidentified assistant on the island (Conrad's original title for the short story was "The Assistant") leads to a series of future deceptions which, though not quite lies, are reticences that allow other people to continue in misunderstandings Renouard knows to be such. The moment Renouard makes that unconsidered decision not to tell his friend the newspaper editor that his assistant has died on the island he begins a destructive collusion with the dead, and eventually dies himself. His fate causes the fate of the silk plants, which start to grow "rank and tall in the deserted fields." But because Conrad sets his story before the results of the fiber tests are known, the story of the plants is more open-ended than the human story: theirs is not a deterministic tale.

This short fiction of Conrad's, with its impressive botanical realism combining with its vacuous story, presents a very useful challenge to the little-scrutinized assumption prevailing with Conrad's fiction generally that there is a strong association between political perspicacity—historical prolepsis—and the value of a work as literary fiction. At the same time, this short story certainly confirms the value of reading Conrad's fiction in reference to historical events before and after the time of his fictional settings, and also after the composition date. The larger-than-life adventure of "Arghan," chronologically postdating Conrad's story of an Arghan-like silk plant, sheds light on the wider continuing story Conrad had tapped into, of useful, potentially transferable, plants capable of producing silk-like fiber.

Acknowledgments

I gratefully acknowledge the generous help of Dr Robert Cribb, Department of Pacific and Asian History, Australian National University, Dr John Loadman, author of *Tears of the Tree* (OUP, 2005), and Dr Mark Nesbitt, Centre for Economic Botany, Royal Botanical Gardens at Kew. I also thank Dr Harry Luther of the Bromeliad Identification Center, Florida.

Notes

1. The best-known case of Conrad's extraordinary percipience about important political matters is his presentation of Belgian King Leopold's hypocritical sanctimonious rapacity in the Congo, in Conrad's short novel "Heart of Darkness" (1899). Francis Ford Coppola based his epic movie *Apocalypse Now* on this same story of Conrad's, relocating it to Vietnam during the 1970s American war. In *Nostromo* (1904), Conrad depicts the activities

of North American business conquistadors and gun-boat paternalism in Panama regions of South America, and *Under Western Eyes* (1910) presents a diagnosis of why democracy was not possible—was institutionally not possible—in Russia. As for *The Secret Agent*, Conrad's novel of 1907 was one of the three works of world fiction most frequently cited in the American media after the terrorist attacks on the United States on September 11, 2001. How central the proleptic claims for his fictions continue to be in contemporary evaluations is amply exemplified in the recent volume *Conrad in the Twenty-First Century: Contemporary Approaches and Perspectives* (Kaplan et al. 2005).

2. P. Colombet, M. Allard, V. Bousquet, C. de Lavigne and P. H. Flurin, "The History of ACL Surgery." http://www.maitrise-orthop.com/corpusmaitri/orthopaedic/87_colombet/colombetus.shtml, accessed July 16, 2007.

3. Cf. esp. Vol.II, Chapter 1, "The Search for Substitutes."

4. Peter Warshall, "Inventory of Synthetic Fibers," *Whole Earth* Summer 1997, at http://www.wholeearthmag.com/ArticleBin/113.html, accessed July 16, 2007.

5. Lawrence Davies says in his note regarding this letter to Pinker, that Conrad was concerned that the Deacon/Deakin likeness might produce problems, Deakin's name being politically topical and relatively well known in England. As to Conrad's motive in changing his character's name, Davies' suggestion is likely to be true, though, in typical Conrad fashion, the actual "model" for old Dunster is probably a plausible intermixture of different real Australian eminents. Conrad's Deacon/Dunster, like many an Australian colonial statesman, had, prior to his retirement, made "a tour in Europe and a lengthy stay in England, during which he had a very good press indeed." His "granting of the Malata concession was the last act of his official life." But long before entering politics this now aged statesman had been a pioneer, like Renouard himself. Dunster had been in his youth a botanical pioneer too, of wheat growing, having showed that it was possible "to raise crops on ground looking barren enough to discourage a magician." The details seem sufficient to give a historical hint as to possible originals for Dunster the elder, at least.

6. http://encarta.msn.com/encyclopedia_761568792.13/Australia.html, accessed July 16, 2007.

7. Sydney *Bulletin*, "Red Page," May 27, 1915.

8. National Archives UK, file on Arghan Fibre, 1919–26. Catalog reference: CO874/950.

9. See also John Loadman, "Sir Henry Alexander Wickham" http://www.bouncing-balls.com/timeline/people/nr_wickham1.htm, accessed July 16, 2007. A biography of Wickham by Joe Jackson is to be published by Viking in 2007.

10. Report of the Extraordinary General Meeting of the Arghan Company Ltd, April 3, 1922, citing a report by Messrs. Wigglesworth and Co., Ltd, Fibre Brokers:

> *Since the collapse of Russia, the world has been deprived of over half a million tons of flax per annum, representing about 70 per cent. of the total flax production of the world. This serious shortage has entirely dislocated the industry, and has led to attempts to substitute various other fibres with indifferent success. The samples of Arghan ... are in my opinion of a quality and a texture to enable this material to be used for heavy counts of yarn in place of either flax or Italian-hemp, and the properties of the fibre as described qualify it to become a substitute for the finer grades of manila used in the manufacture of trawl twines and fishing nets. If your company succeeds in producing on a commercial scale a similar fibre to the sample submitted, there is unquestionably a wide future for it, and there has been no more favourable time in recent years for its introduction to the trade. I should anticipate supplies being absorbed as quickly as they can be produced.*

Also, at the same Extraordinary Meeting, the report of a group

Goulding, Ernest. 1917. *Cotton and Other Vegetable Fibres: Their Production and Utilization*. London: John Murray.

Hanelt, Peter and Institute of Plant Genetics and Crop Plant Research (eds). 2001. *Mansfeld's Encyclopedia of Agricultural and Horticultural Crops*. Berlin: Springer-Verlag.

Kaplan, Carola, Peter Mallios and Andrea White (eds). 2005. *Conrad in the Twenty-First Century: Contemporary Approaches and Perspectives*. New York: Routledge.

Karl, Frederick and Laurence Davies. 1996. *The Collected Letters of Joseph Conrad*, Vol. V. Cambridge: Cambridge University Press.

Lane, E. V. 1953. "Sir Henry Wickham: British Pioneer. A Brief Summary of the Life Story of the British Pioneer Including an Account of the Inception of Plantation Rubber." *Rubber Age* August: 649–56.

Lane, E. V. 1953–4. "The Life and Work of Henry Wickham", *The India-Rubber Journal* (I—"Ancestry and Early Years," December 5, 1953: 14–17; II—"A Journey through the Wilderness," December 12, 1953: 14–18; III—"Santarem," December 19 1953: 18–20; IV—"Kew," December 26, 1953: 5–7; V—"Pioneering in North Queensland," January 2, 1954: 17–19; VI—"Pioneering in British Honduras," January 9, 1954: 17–20; VII—"The Conflict Islands and New Guinea," January 16, 1954: 7–10; VIII—"Piqui-á and Arghan," January 23, 1954: 7–10; IX—"The Closing Years," January 30, 1954: 5–8.)

Loadman, John. 2005. *Tears of the Tree*. Oxford: Oxford University Press.

Merritt Matthews, J. 1916. *The Textile Fibres: Their Physical, Microscopical and Chemical Properties*, 3rd edn. New York: John Wiley & Sons.

Moser, Thomas C. 1966. *Joseph Conrad: Achievement and Decline*. Hamden, CT: Archon Books.

Najder, Zdzisław. 1983. *Joseph Conrad: A Chronicle*. Cambridge: Cambridge University Press.

Said, Edward W. 1966. *Joseph Conrad and the Fiction of Autobiography*, Cambridge, MA: Harvard University Press.

Spruce, Richard. 1908. *Notes of a Botanist on the Amazon & Andes: Being Records of Travel on the Amazon and its Tributaries, the Trombetas, Rio Negro, Uaupés, Casiquiare, Pacimoni, Huallaga, and Pastasa; As Also to the Cataracts of the Orinoco, along the Eastern Side of the Andes of Peru and Ecuador, and the Shores of the Pacific, during the Years 1849–1864*, 2 vols, ed. and condensed by Alfred Russel Wallace. London: Macmillan and Co.

Stockdale, F. A. 1923. "Fibres: Colombian Pita." *The Tropical Agriculturist* LX: 337–45.

Ticktin, Tamara. 2002. "The History of *Ixtle* in Mexico." *Economic Botany* 56(1): 92–4.

Wickham H. A. 1872. *Rough Notes of a Journey through the Wilderness from Trinidad to Para, Brazil by way of the great Cataracts of the Orinoco, Atabapo, and Rio Negro*. London: W. H. J. Carter.

Wickham H. A. 1908. *On the Plantation, Cultivation and Curing of Para Indian Rubber*. London: Kegan Paul, Trench, Trübner & Co.

Wright, C. H. 1923. "Pita and Silk Grass." *Kew Bulletin* 1923: 266–67.

Zanier, Claudio. 2005. "Pre-Modern European Silk Technology and East Asia: Who Imported What?" In Debin Ma (ed.) *Textiles in the Pacific, 1500–1900*, pp. 105–90. Aldershot: Ashgate Publishing.

Returning Navajo-Churro Sheep for Navajo Weaving

Abstract

Navajo-Churro sheep provided a traditional fiber resource for handwoven textiles produced by Navajo people. Sixteenth-century Spanish explorers seeking riches in the American Southwest introduced their Spanish *Churro* sheep, a hardy desert variety whose descendants are the breed known today as Navajo-Churro. As a stable base for Navajo pastoralism, these sheep adapted to the harsh desert landscape of Navajo homelands and provided wealth, food, wool, and social cohesion for the Navajo people. After the mid-nineteenth century when more Anglo-Americans migrated into the Southwest, vast herds of Navajo-Churro sheep were reduced to near extinction through outright destruction and by crossbreeding with high-production breeds. During the 1970s, Navajo and non-Navajo herders and weavers joined in coordinated efforts to return the Navajo-Churro breed to Navajo lands and people. The contemporary Navajo organization *Diné be' iiná* (abbreviated to DBI and translated as The Navajo Lifeway) provided leadership for the return of Navajo-Churro sheep. In this article, we explore how the return of Navajo-Churro sheep and wool can strengthen cultural identity, rekindle ideological teachings, and revitalize material culture. The analysis provides an example of development intervention at the level of raw materials, as opposed to design, product development, or marketing intercession with textile traditions.

Keywords: Navajo, sheep, weaving, wool, cultural identity, local breed

SUSAN M. STRAWN AND MARY A. LITTRELL

Susan M. Strawn is Assistant Professor in the Department of Apparel Design and Merchandising at Dominican University in River Forest, Illinois. She received her doctoral degree in textiles and clothing from Iowa State University. Her teaching and research interests include cultural and historical analysis of twentieth-century textiles and dress, artisan sustainability, and surface design of hand-produced textiles.

Mary A. Littrell received her doctoral degree from Purdue University and is Professor and Chair of the Department of Design and Merchandising at Colorado State University. Her teaching and research scholarship focus on alternative/fair trade, marketing systems for cultural products, artisan enterprise performance and sustainability, tourism, and ethnographic textiles and dress. She is co-author, with Marsha A. Dickson, of *Social Responsibility in the Global Market: Fair Trade of Cultural Products*.

Returning Navajo-Churro Sheep for Navajo Weaving

Introduction

The Navajo people have gained renown for their handwoven tapestry textiles. The greatest concentration of Navajo weavers today is on the Navajo Nation (Figure 1), a reservation on a portion of the traditional Navajo homelands in the southwestern United States. Nearly 300,000 Navajo people live in small population centers or isolated housing clusters on the 17-million-acre (26,000 square miles) reservation sprawling across Arizona, New Mexico, and Utah (Choudhary 2000, 2003; Goodman 1982). It is generally accepted that bands of hunting and gathering Athapaskan people, the ancestral Navajos and Apaches, migrated from Canada and established clan-based family clusters in southwestern North America by the early sixteenth century (Towner 1996; Wheat 2003). In contrast, Puebloan people were well established in this region for at least 1,000 years before the Athapaskans arrived. During the early eighteenth century, the Navajo population emerged as a distinct culture, described as a "biological and cultural hybrid(s), neither Athapaskan nor Puebloan, but a product of both" (Bailey and Bailey 1986: 15). The Navajo people often refer to themselves as *Diné* (The People).

The Navajo Nation is the context for this article and for the interpretive study with *Diné be' iiná* (abbreviated to DBI, translated as The Navajo Lifeway), a contemporary nonprofit Navajo organization that works to restore the Navajo-Churro breed of sheep. Building upon participatory research and collaboration with DBI across four years, the authors examined inductively those components of Navajo cultural identity linked with Navajo-Churro sheep and wool. Two initial questions provided context for analysis: what historical relationships can be identified between Navajo-Churro sheep and the Navajo people? Which characteristics of Navajo-Churro sheep and wool have influenced Navajo weaving? We then asked: what linkages may emerge among Navajo-Churro sheep, Navajo textiles, and Navajo cultural identity?

Artisan Sustainability

Understanding factors that contribute to artisan sustainability is of critical importance to the world's artisans who depend on hand-produced textiles for their economic livelihood and for whom textile production is closely intertwined with cultural identity. Scholars and development organizations argue the relative merits of factors used to assess progress toward sustainable development. Raw materials available to artisans, in particular traditional fiber resources with multi-generational links to cultural

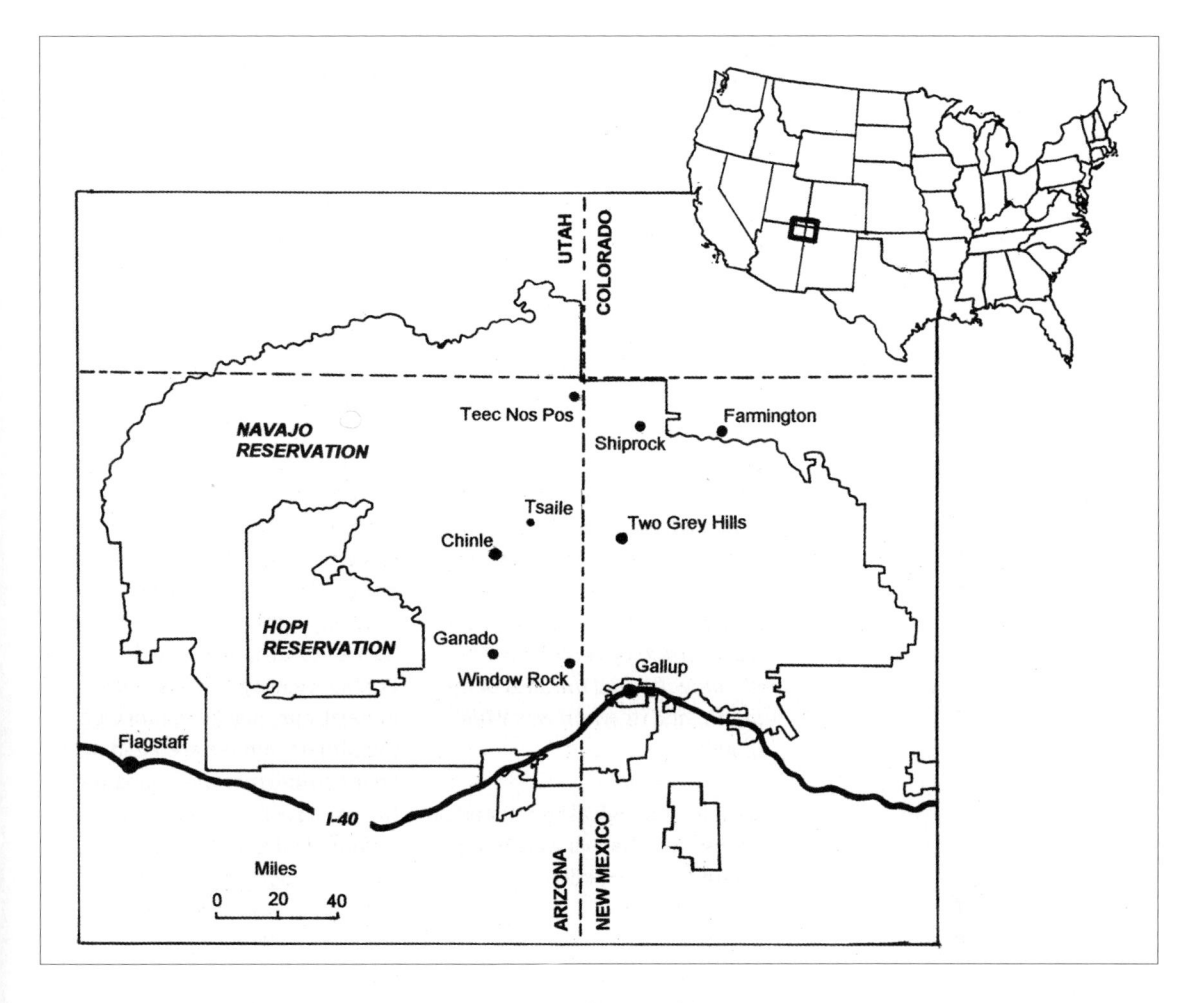

Figure 1
Map of the contemporary Navajo Nation. Illustration by Susan M. Strawn.

identity, are one factor with the potential to influence sustainable development for artisans. Empirical evidence about fiber resources can inform arguments about sustainable development intervention strategies.

Much of the scholarly dialogue about textile artisans and sustainability has concentrated on introduction of business skills, design, and product development, often emphasizing global market profitability and artisan empowerment (Littrell and Dickson 1999). Rather, in this analysis we explore how intervention at the level of a raw material may contribute to strengthening cultural identity through renewed social integration, rekindled ideological teachings, and revitalized material culture.[1] The significance of Navajo-Churro wool as a raw material used for Navajo weaving has received relatively little attention.

Navajo Weaving

Handwoven tapestry textiles have earned widespread recognition for Navajo weavers, who adopted a vertical-style loom, presumably acquired from the Puebloans of the Colorado Plateau (Teague 1998; Wheat 2003). Weavers may be quick to point out, however, that most weavers among Puebloan people are men, while Navajo weavers are usually women. Also, according to Navajo origin stories

Spider Man and Woman introduced weaving to the Navajos:

Spider Woman instructed the Navajo women how to weave on a loom which Spider Man told them how to make. The crosspoles were made of sky and earth cords, the warp sticks of sun rays, the healds [heddles] of rock crystal and sheet lightning. The batten was a sun halo, white shell made the comb. There were four spindles: one a stick of zigzag lightning with a whorl of cannel coal; one a stick of flash lightning with a whorl of turquoise; a third had a stock of sheet lightning with a whorl of abalone; a rain streamer formed the stick of the south, and its whorl was white shell.[2]

Extant archeological and historical textiles show Navajo weavers acquired superb skills with complex weaving techniques, including diagonal and diamond twill weave. Though considerable variations occur over time and among individual weavers, a characteristic Navajo handwoven textile is woven vertically from the bottom upwards in a tight weft-faced plain tapestry weave with tightly tied selvedge corners and self-tassels (Figure 2). Characteristic warp selvedge consists of a selvedge braid with two three-ply, twined cords; weft selvedge is a single outside warp cord or a selvedge braid with two three-ply, twined cords (Wheat 2003). The earliest Navajo weaving designs show the same horizontal striping found in Pueblo weaving. Navajo weaving innovations, however, broke up the stripes into terraced geometric shapes similar to that found on Navajo baskets produced well before blankets were woven (Wheat 2003).

Figure 2
Detail of contemporary, Klagatoh-style Navajo handwoven rug showing weft salvage. Photograph by Susan M. Strawn.

The earliest known fragments of Navajo weaving date to the late eighteenth and early nineteenth centuries. One fragment excavated from Massacre Cave is a section of a wearing blanket woven of handspun wool with a white ground and stripes in a range of natural colors (Kluckhohn et al. 1971). In addition to various styles of wearing blankets, Navajo weavers have created such practical woolen pieces as saddle blankets, ponchos, sarapes, and one- and two-piece dresses. Although styles varied by region, the most common woolen dress worn during the nineteenth century was made from two rectangular blankets sewn together down the sides and across the shoulders, leaving head and arm openings (Figure 3). A woven belt with fringe tied the dress at the waist. A less common style of woolen dress, similar to the Puebloan style, consisted of one woven blanket folded and sewn down most of one side and across one end, leaving openings for head and one arm. Women draped this style under the right shoulder and over the left, catching it at the waist with a belt. Both dress styles reached to the lower leg and were often plain black or indigo blue, although many had horizontal stripes of colors woven into the borders. By the early twentieth century, women no longer wove or wore these dresses (Kluckhohn et al. 1971; Wheat 2003).

Eyewitness accounts date Navajo weaving for trade with the Pueblos and Spanish settlements to the eighteenth century. Patterns of trade and the advent of tourism to the Southwest led to the transformation of Navajo wearing blankets and dresses into rugs and wall hangings marketed to non-Navajo consumers. Figure 2, for example, shows a detail of a Navajo tapestry twill wall hanging woven in the Klagetoh regional style with a red color associated with the Ganado region. Subsequent development of weaving techniques, regional styles, and chronology of Navajo weaving are extensively documented (Amsden 1934; Bennett and Bighorse 1971; Blomberg 1988; Franciscan Fathers 1910; Hedlund 1990; Kahlenberg and Berlant 1972; Kent 1985; Matthews 1884; Reichard 1984[1936]; Rodee 1995; Wheat 2003).

"Old Navajo Sheep"

The story of sheep, Navajo culture, and weaving begins with accounts of Spanish explorers in the American Southwest. In 1540, rumors of great riches lured Francisco de Coronado and his extensive entourage into the Southwest, bringing thousands of sheep intended for meat, not wool. Subsequently, Spaniards claimed and colonized the land, and in 1598 Don Juan Oñate introduced the first sheep intended to be used for wool as well as food—Churro sheep, the desert sheep of southern Spain (Wheat 2003). Spain had exported only a few of their famous fine-wooled Merino sheep to New Spain, but none were introduced into the American Southwest until the nineteenth century. The Spanish Churro is the foundation

Figure 3
Stereoscopic images of Navajo woman shown wearing a *bil* (dress) in an 1878 studio portrait. Photograph © Denver Public Library, Western History Collection, James Thurlow, X-33004.

breed for the sheep referred to as "Old Navajo Sheep" and known today as the Navajo-Churro breed.

Historical accounts document sheep in Navajo possession as early as 1640. Navajo people obtained sheep from Spanish and Puebloan people either through trading or by capturing livestock during retaliatory raids (Bailey 1980; Wheat 2003). Women in matrilineal Navajo culture were the traditional owners of sheep (Bailey 1980; Towner 1996; Wheat 2003). Children were given responsibility for herding sheep at very young ages, often as early as five years. When parents and elders taught children to care for the sheep, they also educated children into the Navajo lifeway. Herding was a "central part of the Navajo socialization process" (Iverson 1981: 7).

Navajo-Churro Sheep, a Local Breed

Over time, the sheep owned by the Navajo people have included the Old Navajo Sheep (Navajo-Churro); such introduced high-production breeds as Merino, Rambouillet, and Karakul; and the resulting crossbred sheep. Navajo-Churro sheep, however, hold historical importance as the first Navajo sheep, aesthetic value for textile production, sacred meaning in Navajo origin stories (Reichard 1934), and ecological worth as a "local" breed. During the approximate 10,000 years since humans first domesticated livestock from wild species, the majority of breeds have been associated with specific cultures and environments. Such local breeds developed disease resistance and made more efficient use of resources in marginal environments that account for two-thirds of the world's land surface (Geerlings et al. 2002; Köhler-Rollefson 2001). During the twentieth century, however, Westernized agricultural practices reversed the emphasis on local breeds. Instead, agricultural methods promoted a small number of high-performance (improved) breeds considered superior for greater production of meat and wool within controlled environments (Heise and Christman 1989; Sponenberg and Bixby 2000). These marketing strategies encouraged raising a few improved breeds and threatened the survival of such local breeds as the Navajo-Churro, as well as the isolated cultures that have depended on local breeds in the past:

Navajo-Churro sheep are a good example of a breed shaped by close interaction with humans in a challenging environment. As mainstream America hurried down its path to prosperity and success, many cultures and situations in isolated regions were simply left out, to varying degrees. This resulted in little appreciation for these sheep, for their role in their original location, and for the products they offered. (Sponenberg and Bixby 2000: 17)

As a local breed, Navajo-Churro sheep have adapted to the desert and canyon terrain of the Navajo Nation. Improved sheep are larger, wider, heavier animals bred to support greater weight and wool yields. By contrast, Navajo-Churro are small sheep with the narrow bodies, long legs, and light bones appropriate for walking long distances to graze on arid lands. Faces, legs, and bellies have little fleece to snag on spines of desert plants (Figure 4). The smaller stature combined with a lower wool yield (four to five pounds) in comparison with a high-production breed (eight to twelve pounds) enable Navajo-Churro sheep to eat less. They are also disease resistant. Known for high fecundity, Navajo-Churro ewes mature early, lamb relatively easily, often produce twins and triplets, and protect their lambs aggressively (Blunn 1943; Heise and Christman 1989; N-CSA 2006). The Navajo-Churro is an ideally suited breed for harsh range and climate conditions of the Navajo Nation.

Navajo-Churro Wool

Navajo-Churro wool has qualities characteristic of a local breed, distinctly different from that of improved breeds. The wool of improved breeds is suitable for commercial production and weaving fine cloth, but Navajo-Churro wool is ideal for hand production and Navajo weaving. Unlike improved breeds selectively bred for a coat of predominantly fine white wool preferred by

Figure 4
Navajo-Churro ewe with characteristic scant fleece on face and legs. Photograph by Susan M. Strawn.

Figure 5
A variety of natural colors found among Navajo-Churro sheep. Photograph by Susan M. Strawn.

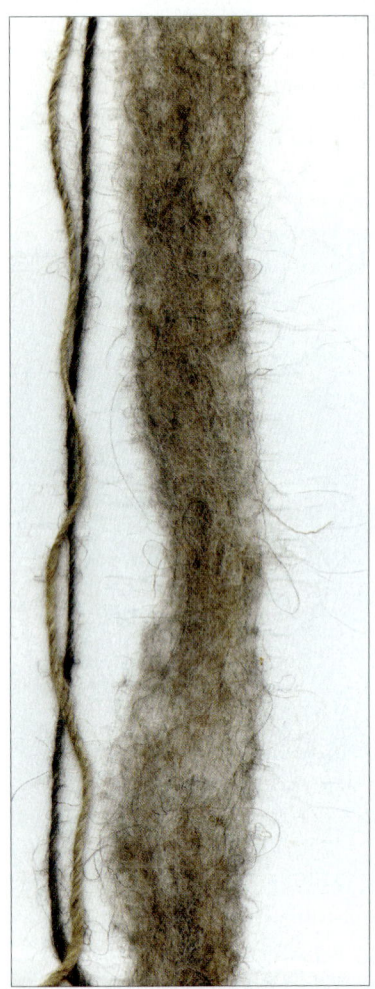

Figure 6
Navajo-Churro carded wool and handspun yarn in natural colors show long hair fibers, short wool fibers, and the kemp characteristic of the Navajo-Churro breed. Photograph by Susan M. Strawn.

commercial dyeing and textile industries, the colors of the Navajo-Churro coat—creamy white, black, light tan, gray, blue-gray, brown, red-brown, and multicolored—reflect the adaptation of their wild or feral ancestors for concealment (Figure 5). While improved breeds have fine wool fibers, Navajo-Churro wool has retained the double coat characteristic of unimproved breeds: an outer coat of long, coarse hair fibers, an inner coat of short finer wool fiber, plus a variable amount of kemp (hair) fibers (Figure 6). Fibers of this type can be easily hand-carded and spun into yarn on a Navajo spindle, and contribute high durability and luster to Navajo handwoven textiles (Figure 7).

Wool from improved and crossbred sheep is fine and short-stapled with heavy crimp and high grease content, a combination of traits that is more difficult to hand-card and spin into suitable yarn for Navajo weaving (Bailey 1980; Reichard 1984[1936]). Navajo-Churro wool has the low grease content of their desert ancestors; their wool repels sand and dust during desert windstorms. Cleaner wool may not require washing, a distinct advantage in a land of scarce water. Fleece from some Navajo-Churro ewes can be spun without carding, another quality that takes the weaver from fleece to loom more quickly. Navajo-Churro wool—coarse, long staple, low crimp, low grease—is well suited for Navajo textile production (Blunn 1940, 1943; Grandstaff 1942; Heise and Christman 1989; Phillips 1941; Wheat 2003).

Loss of Navajo Sheep

Navajo-Churro wool predominates in Navajo textiles until around 1870 (Blomberg 1988; Wheat 2003). Over time, the opportunity to work with Navajo-Churro wool slipped away from Navajo weavers. The

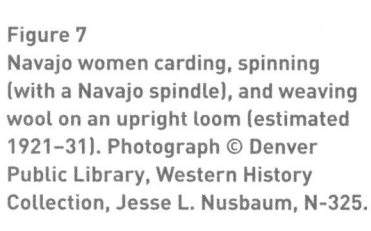

Figure 7
Navajo women carding, spinning (with a Navajo spindle), and weaving wool on an upright loom (estimated 1921–31). Photograph © Denver Public Library, Western History Collection, Jesse L. Nusbaum, N-325.

numbers of Navajo-Churro sheep were reduced from the countless hundreds of thousands observed mid-nineteenth century to near extinction in the twentieth century. Threats to Navajo pastoralism began soon after the Mexican-American War when in 1848, New Mexico was ceded to the United States and more Anglo-Americans moved into the Southwest. Beginning in 1863, Navajo sheep were destroyed as part of a federal scorched-earth campaign to subdue Navajo people and remove them from their traditional homelands. Navajo people were encouraged to surrender, many with their livestock, for the 300-mile forced removal—the Navajo Long Walk—to Bosque Redondo, New Mexico (Fort Sumner). Following confinement under tragic conditions, a federal treaty of 1868 reestablished the Navajo tribe on a portion of their home country, though within defined boundaries.

The treaty also specified that Navajo survivors be given New Mexican sheep, descendents of the Spanish Churro. An unknown number of Navajo sheep had survived in the remote canyons of Navajo lands (Bailey 1964; Blunn 1940). Reservation Agents, however, attempted to increase wool yield and meat production by crossbreeding the Navajo sheep with high-production breeds. Though well intended, crossbreeding led to "genetic chaos" in Navajo flocks (Bailey and Bailey 1986: 131).

After Fort Sumner, the heart of Navajo economy was livestock. Dramatic increases in the crossbred sheep population precipitated federal livestock reductions begun in 1934. Destruction of livestock, including small flocks of the remaining Navajo-Churro sheep, shocked the Navajo people, who plunged into poverty (Bailey 1980; Iverson

1981). During the same time, the federal government recognized the critical role of weaving—and supplies of suitable wool—within the Navajo economy. To address this need, in 1936 the government initiated the Southwestern Range and Sheep Breeding Laboratory (SRSBL) as part of the Depression-era New Deal. Although charged with identifying improved breeds best suited to crossbreed with Navajo-Churro, SRSBL animal scientists recommended selective breeding of Navajo-Churro sheep to produce the most suitable fleece qualities preferred by Navajo weavers. Nevertheless, crossbred sheep with wool unsuitable for either commercial or traditional hand textile production continued to predominate on the reservation (Blunn 1940, 1943; Grandstaff 1942).[3]

After the Second World War, the isolation of the Navajo people lessened. Road construction, wage labor, mandatory education, and off-reservation travel increased contact between Navajo and Anglo people and cultures. As a result, the Navajo Nation economy shifted from subsistence agriculture that included sheep and wool, to a wage, welfare, and informal (self-employed) economy based in such natural resources as timber and coal (Choudhary 2000, 2003). The numbers of Navajo-Churro sheep plunged further. By the 1970s, the American Livestock Breeds Conservancy (ALBC), a not-for-profit organization that protects domesticated livestock breeds, estimated that no more than 450 Navajo-Churro sheep survived (2004).

Returning Navajo-Churro Sheep
In the 1970s, Navajo and non-Navajo individuals, through coordinated efforts, began to locate, breed, and restore Navajo-Churro sheep to Navajo lands and people, and to a growing consumer fiber handcraft market with an interest in natural fibers. The Navajo Sheep Project (NSP) at Utah State University, foremost among these efforts, established breeding lines of Navajo-Churro sheep derived from small numbers of old-type Navajo sheep purchased from Navajo women living in isolated regions of the reservation. The NSP built a substantial breeding herd of Navajo-Churro sheep and returned the majority to selected herding and weaving families on the Navajo Nation (McNeal 1986). In 1986, fiber handcraft and wool specialists established the Navajo-Churro Sheep Association (N-CSA), based on breed standards delineated by the ALBC. In 1991, the NSP served as the umbrella organization for founding *Diné be' iiná* (DBI) as a community-based organization focused on restoring Navajo-Churro sheep (ALBC 2006; Diné be' iiná 2002a, b, 2004; N-CSA 2006). In 2002, DBI formed a 501(c)(3) charitable and educational organization granted under the Navajo Nation Nonprofit Act. The course of this article will summarize interpretive research conducted with Diné be' iiná.[4]

***Diné be' iiná* (Navajo Lifeway)**
Diné be' iiná (DBI) works to restore Navajo-Churro sheep and to support culturally relevant economic development based on sheep, wool, and fiber arts. The majority of members active with DBI during the time of the study were college-educated volunteers, and all members spoke fluent English. Grants, volunteers, and *pro bono* consultants supported the majority of DBI programs and activities. Governing executive and advisory boards organized educational programs and events that emphasized ways to restore Navajo-Churro sheep, manage range and grazing, encourage youth involvement, generate income with small flocks, and experience hands-on training and knowledge. The Articles of Incorporation summarize the purpose of the organization:

The statement of the character of the affairs of the Corporation is to train, educate, and develop the capacity of Navajo communities and persons to preserve and continue their culture, traditions and livelihood, in particular, those that sheep, wool and weaving have meant, and continue to mean, to the Diné. (Diné be' iiná, 2002a: Article IV)

The Sheep is Life Celebration (SiLC), the major annual event sponsored by DBI, "honor(s) the central role that sheep play in Navajo spirituality, philosophy, and daily life" (Diné be' iiná 2004). Held on the Navajo Nation, pre-celebration workshops with hands-on instruction in Navajo fiber techniques precede two days of presentations and discussions about economic development and value-added marketing, range and livestock management, arts and crafts sales, micro-enterprise, and both traditional and innovative applications of wool to fiber arts. The concurrent livestock show includes competitions that recognize and reward superior quality Navajo-Churro sheep and fleece, a primary way to improve the breed. In 2006, a series of mini-Sheep is Life events were held at different locations throughout the year on the Navajo Nation in place of the single annual event.

Collaboration with *Diné be' iiná* offered opportunities to explore factors of cultural identity associated with organized efforts to reintroduce Navajo-Churro sheep for Navajo weaving. Research focused on interviews with DBI members and participation in events DBI organized on and near the Navajo Nation from 2001 to 2004. In-depth interviews included all DBI leaders at the time. DBI workshops and educational events were open to Navajo and non-Navajo participants alike, and participation deepened understanding of the importance of Navajo-Churro sheep and fleece to the DBI mission and in Navajo wool processing and weaving. Photography and field notes recorded details of the sheep and wool competitions, weaving, and other activities.

Material Culture

In this article, we adopted the conceptualization that culture embraces social behavior in the form of normative patterns of action, ideology as overarching beliefs and values, and the material artifacts and natural environment that surround everyday life (Ferraro 1998). Research results related to the material culture component of cultural identity tended to predominate. Simply owning Navajo-Churro sheep emerged as a strong component of cultural identity. "It was the return of the Churro sheep, to have been part of that and continuing to reintroduce the Churro sheep back to some more people who don't have that," said a weaver who had assumed responsibility for the family Navajo-Churro flock, "That was, for me, the most positive thing that I've seen" (01).[5] Navajo elders in particular who had "thought that the [Navajo-Churro] sheep would never come back, that it was gone, was extinct" (13) expressed emotional reactions:

I remember when we first brought our sheep back. My sister had this sheep for a while, and then we had this grandpa that lived way across from us. One day he came over to visit, and he was sitting behind the shade house. I said, "Why are you crying for, grandpa?" He said, "It's been a long time since I've seen these sheep. I'm so happy that they're here again." (14)

In the past, owning Navajo-Churro sheep meant economic independence. A sheep producer with a flock of about 200 Navajo-Churro recalled his grandfather had said, "The sheep will always be there for you. No matter what. Through thick and thin the sheep will be there for you. A job can disappear years down the road. The sheep will still be there for you" (09). The mother of a weaver who raises Navajo-Churro warned, "not to ever let go of the sheep, because without sheep there's no stability in your life ... Without sheep, you're in poverty" (01).

The unique qualities of Navajo-Churro wool—natural colors and fleece properties—appeared linked with the material culture component of cultural identity. Weavers and wool producers alike embraced the unique natural colors and fleece qualities of Navajo-Churro wool as well suited for Navajo weaving. Weavers in particular praised the natural colors of Navajo-Churro fleece. A weaver with relatives from Two Gray Hills, a regional style characterized by the sole use of natural colors, said the advantage of Navajo-Churro wool is "the colors, that beautiful rich red brown ... Maybe some other breeds can achieve those colors, but we already have Churro sheep that have those colors. They're just so beautiful" (08). Another weaver who had used commercial colors in the past said her "children introduced me to this [Navajo-Churro] wool. Oh, wow! This is so beautiful, and it's natural ... And I just fell in love with it" (07). A DBI leader who had purchased her first Navajo-Churro sheep wanted to be known for breeding shades of brown, "to specialize in brown sheep, tan sheep, rust-colored sheep" (04). During the wool judging competition at the 2005 Sheep is Life Celebration, the first placed fleece showed outstanding even and dense color saturation (Lyle McNeal, personal communication, June 24, 2005).

Navajo-Churro fleece has other distinctive characteristics, in addition to the range of natural colors. Churro wool differs along breeding lines and among individual sheep according to age, region, and weather conditions. At the 2005 SiLC, the Navajo-Churro fleece awarded first place was soft, bulky, and low in grease with a long staple, less than two percent kemp, and a good balance between coarse outer coat and fine inner coat. Tips were not fused, and the fleece was not tangled or brittle (Lyle McNeal, personal communication, June 24, 2005).

Interestingly, weavers often mentioned family elders who had kept small flocks of old-type Navajo sheep specifically for wool for weaving. Although Navajo-Churro sheep had been crossbred with high-production breeds since the mid-1800s, interview data suggested that weavers had retained and refused to crossbreed small flocks of pure Navajo-Churro sheep. One weaver, for example, said her grandmother "kept her own little herd of Churro ... She wove, so she used that in her weaving. The other weavers in the area came to her for that particular fleece" (09). These were presumably the source of Navajo-Churro sheep that seeded the Navajo Sheep Project.

Over time, many Navajo weavers have lost the traditional knowledge of techniques needed to process fleece with Navajo-Churro qualities. Weavers have assimilated a sophisticated range of raw materials, in place of or in addition to wool from Navajo-Churro sheep, into their weaving and yet continued to create textiles easily recognized as Navajo (Hedlund 2003). Interestingly, DBI members had learned more about wool processing than any other skill gained since they joined the organization. Several weavers had "learned to go back to carding and spinning the wool instead of going to Griswell [a pawn shop that sells commercial yarn]" (05). Non-Navajo commercial markets have held Navajo-Churro fleece in low regard, an opinion that appeared to permeate the attitude of Navajo sheep producers and weavers. The descendent of a prominent weaving family said, "My grandparents were told it [Navajo-Churro fleece] was low quality wool ... They lost the knack of working with Churro wool." She agreed the coarse fiber can be hard to work with, but added, "There are ways of working with Churro wool. That has to be relearned" (09). Two weavers had taught their mothers to hand-spin Navajo-Churro wool using a Navajo spindle. One said her mother "thinks they [Navajo-Churro sheep] have coarse, tough wool." She told her mother that those are the older sheep, that "if you get some younger ones and start shearing them, then tell the difference." She had decided that, "I'm sort of teaching her, and she's willing, too" (04). A non-weaver who did not own Navajo-Churro sheep perhaps summarized an overall attitude toward Navajo-Churro wool:

In school, we're taught the fine wool breeds have the biggest market because they produce very good products ... But I guess quality has different meanings. To us, the Navajo-Churro wool is very valuable. We see it as higher quality. We would rather have Navajo-Churro wool, a coarser wool, than a fine wool because we want our rugs to endure anything they're exposed to in the environment ... We use a lot of Churro wool to make the rugs because they're a lot more durable, and they can handle a lot more wear and tear over the years. (11)

Two weavers owned Navajo-Churro sheep whose fleece could be hand-spun without carding. Both acknowledged historical precedence for this practice, consistent with the observations of Reichard (1984[1936]). "A lot of people, the older folks, they remember," said one weaver. "They say you can just spin when you shear" (13). The other weaver had two ewes with fleece that did not need carding, so "you just go straight to spinning. By not carding them you don't agitate the fiber at all and you don't make them rough" (09). Although Navajo weaving techniques remain virtually unchanged, many weavers have welcomed new equipment—drum carders and spinning wheels, in particular—that speed the carding and spinning process. A weaver observed, "A lot of our people ... have benefited, ... are able to see these new inventions that will help us get faster to the loom" (08). Consistent with Ferraro's model of culture, weavers and sheep producers alike described Navajo-Churro sheep and wool as components of their material cultural identity. The sheep themselves and the unique colors and fleece qualities are material artifacts and part of the natural environment that can surround the lives of weavers.

Ideology, Values, and Beliefs

Although data about material culture components of cultural identity tended to predominate, ideological components associated with beliefs and values emerged from research nearly as often. Ideological components related to cultural identity were linked with the need to restore awareness of the historical, sacred, and ecological value of Navajo-Churro sheep within Navajo culture. Much of this awareness had been lost among Navajo people in general. To a DBI member in her twenties, gaining awareness meant that, "we do have something worth holding onto in our culture ... Things that our ancestors did we can still do today. It's something that is alive right now" (11). Although off-reservation woolen mills had rejected the coarse wool of Navajo-Churro sheep, awareness of their history could affect a change of heart about Navajo-Churro sheep. A DBI member who held a poor opinion of Navajo-Churro sheep before joining the organization said, "When I look back on the history, there's a profound respect for the sheep, and they contributed to that history" (12).

Equally important to the awareness of history was awareness of the sacred value of Navajo-Churro sheep as the "spiritual sheep for the Navajo people" (01). Navajo legend depicts Navajo-Churro fleece as "the cloud that was talked about in the creation of the sheep, when the cloud was then taken down and formed into the sheep. That's what it is to us. It's not just yarn and fiber. It's meaningful" (01). Another weaver knew that Navajo-Churro sheep had their own chant, supposedly established before the Spaniards brought the Churro sheep. According to legend, the Navajo people "were separated from this animal and the weaving. Then they were reunited" (09). In contrast, awareness of the ecological suitability of Navajo-Churro sheep was seldom mentioned during interviews. Educational programs included topics about ecological fit, however, and a sheep producer acknowledged the breed as "better adapted to the area" and "more valuable" for higher survival rate of lambs (13).

Normative Behavior and Social Cohesion

Additional components linked with cultural identity were related to normative or expected patterns of action, in particular those that a traditional fiber resource and Navajo cultural identity. The Ferraro (1998) conceptualization of culture adopted for this analysis provided a model for organizing cultural identity according to material artifacts, ideology as overarching beliefs and values, and normative or expected patterns of action.

Navajo-Churro sheep are a traditional part of Navajo material culture. Ownership of Navajo-Churro sheep in itself reinforces cultural identity among sheep producers and weavers involved with restoration of the sheep to the Navajo Nation. The range of natural colors and unique fleece qualities are well suited for Navajo weaving. Selective breeding of Navajo-Churro sheep on the reservation has provided another choice of fiber and yarn, a choice with cultural relevance. Owning the sheep has also returned control of a fiber resource to the weavers, providing insulation from outside market price fluctuations and decreasing dependence on outside control of the availability of raw materials. Returning Navajo-Churro sheep also ensures a culturally authentic resource essential for the repair and conservation of certain vintage Navajo textiles.

The history of Navajo-Churro sheep is intimately linked with the history of the Navajo people. The sheep have also occupied a significant place in Navajo creation stories and spirituality. The ideological components of cultural identity focus on regaining awareness of historical, sacred, and ecological place of Navajo-Churro sheep within Navajo culture. The history and sacred nature of the sheep, however, tended to overshadow their value as a local breed. Those cultural components associated with normative or expected patterns of behavior appeared linked with social cohesion. Individual fidelity to pastoral heritage within a family encouraged multi-generational cohesion, including concern for youth. In the past, elders and parents relied on caring for sheep as a traditional way to teach children valuable life lessons embedded in Navajo culture. Preserving Navajo-Churro sheep as a local breed also encouraged the preservation of traditional knowledge associated with caring for the breed and weaving with the wool. Returning Navajo-Churro sheep appeared to support the matrilineal aspect of Navajo culture and persistence of fluency in the Navajo language, especially through communication between youth and elders. For Navajo weavers, the material, ideological, and social linkages between Navajo-Churro sheep and cultural identity may contribute to artisan sustainability and the survival of Navajo weaving.

Notes

1. In this article we adopt a conceptualization of culture that embraces social behavior in the form of normative or expected patterns of action, ideology as a group's overarching beliefs and values, and the material artifacts and natural environment surrounding everyday life (Ferraro 1998).
2. This account of Spider Man and Spider Woman is recorded in *The Navajo Blanket* (Kahlenberg and Berlant 1972).

3. Introduced materials made it possible for weavers to bypass the labor-intensive steps of shearing, wool processing, spinning, washing, and dyeing that require more time than weaving. In the past, sheep were shorn with hand shears or shearing knife, though shearers today often use electric shears. Shorn fleece is sorted for use, with wool from the back and sides preferred for spinning into yarn. Hand-carders—wooden paddles with wire teeth—are used to align wool fibers. Carders were likely adopted from the Spanish, obtained later from Indian agents, and may be replaced by mechanical drum carders today. The characteristic Navajo lap spindle imparts a Z-spun twist when wool fibers are drawn out and turned counterclockwise to form thick roving. The spinner reattaches and spins the roving as many times as necessary, usually two or three times, to create the thickness of yarn desired for weft yarns and as many as six times for warp yarns that require greater strength. Today spinners may also use a variety of commercial spinning wheels, although early observers noted that Navajo spinners rejected Anglo-introduced wheels (Franciscan Fathers 1910; Wheat 2003).

4. This study used an interpretive (naturalistic) research design, appropriate for studies that attempt to see the world from the viewpoint of people who participate in the study and to capture ways that people construct meanings and define their world (Lincoln and Guba 1985). Research carried out on the Navajo Nation included participant observation at DBI workshops, meetings, and events; in-depth, ethnographic interviews with a purposive sample of DBI membership; and field notes and photography. Participant observation, document analysis, supporting interviews, and in-depth participant interviews provided quantitative and qualitative data for analysis and reporting (Glaser 1992; Glaser and Strauss 1967). Triangulating multiple data sources established validity; consistent transcription of interviews, observational field notes, establishment of inter-rater reliability, and participant member checks contributed to reliability (Lincoln and Guba 1985). Data analysis procedures, based on the constant comparative methods of coding and interpretation of data, began after the first interview and continued throughout the collection (Glaser 1992; Glaser and Strauss 1967). Major and minor themes were identified as they emerged from interview data. Participant observations in field notes, evidence from supporting interviews and documents, and interview responses were searched for the most salient data that informed each theme. Four overarching major themes demonstrated that DBI uses educational channels to promote the restoration of Navajo-Churro sheep and wool as a component of Navajo cultural identity and for traditional Navajo cultural products.

5. The number within parentheses represents the code number for the participant who provided the quotation. Code numbers assure anonymity for participants and demonstrate that data analysis drew from a range of participants.

References

ALBC. 2006. American Livestock Breeds Conservancy. http://www.albc-usa.org/, accessed May 10, 2006.

Amsden, C. A. 1934. *Navajo Weaving: Its Technique and History*. Santa Anna, CA: Fine Arts Press.

Bailey, L. R. 1964. *The Long Walk: A History of the Navajo Wars, 1846–68*. Pasadena, CA: Socio-Technical Books.

Bailey, G. 1980. *If You Take My Sheep—: The Evolution and Conflicts of Navajo Pastoralism, 1630–1868*. Pasadena, CA: Westernlore Publications.

Bailey, G. and Bailey, R. G. 1986. *A History of the Navajos: The Reservation Years*. Santa Fe, NM: School of American Research Press.

Bennett, N. and Bighorse, T. 1971. *Working with the Wool: How to Weave a Navajo Rug*. Flagstaff, AZ: Northland Press.

Blomberg, N. J. 1988. *Navajo Textiles: The William Randolph Hearst Collection*. Tucson, AZ: University of Arizona Press.

Blunn, C. T. 1940. "Improvement of the Navajo Sheep." *Journal of Heredity* 31(3): 98–112.

Figure 1
Diane Samuels. Detail view from inside "Lines of Sight," looking through lenses, glass disks, prisms, and engraved lines of poetry. "Lines of Sight," Sidney E. Frank Hall for Life Sciences at Brown University.

Figure 2
Diane Samuels. View from outside of "Lines of Sight." "Lines of Sight," Sidney E. Frank Hall for Life Sciences at Brown University.

over time and through space. The details in "Lines of Sight" and the multiple layers of meaning within it unfold as time is spent exploring and experiencing the work. All of Samuels' works take the viewer on a journey. This bridge, this mode of transportation, also informs the link between different types of human creative endeavor and their meaning.

Samuels often begins her art-making process by researching and interviewing the people engaged in the institution that has commissioned her, doing the intellectual work where she has been engaged to make a site-specific work. In this case, she began by investigating the strategies and processes used by scientists. Interested in discovering how scientists see the world and how they describe it, she wanted to see if there might be a connection to her practice as an artist.

After interviewing life scientists in research laboratories in both Pittsburgh and Providence, she focused on this similarity: artists and scientists both actively observe, scrutinize and evaluate the world. "The scientists spoke about the necessity of looking closely, of penetrating layers, of trying to find the smallest element. Whether the smallest element was a cell, an amino acid, or a molecule, they said they always had to understand it as part of a larger organism." Samuels translated these ideas into a visual form using glass and text. Arranging a multitude of glass elements into a tapestry of glass disks and horizontal bands with text, the glass bridge is a curtain wall—enhancing and obscuring the view inside and outside the bridge.

"Lines of Sight" contains 650,000 glass elements including distillation and prismatic beads, mirrors, and lenses with varying levels of magnification. These lenses function as occuli creating an infinite number of visual experiences. The viewer has the choice of focusing on a detail in the wall of glass: they could focus on a pattern in the glass, observe a reflection in a mirrored lens, or read the etched texts; or the viewer can look through the glass wall to the world outside. Viewed through a prism or a magnifier, the exterior is enlarged or rendered minute. Samuels, by inserting these special little visual moments, alters viewers' perception of the real world. This is the magic of art (and science). It reveals something new, something previously unseen, and demonstrates the ways in which discovery is a domain of both art and science.

Samuels says that her many years of experience working with textiles provided the foundation and familiarity that allows her to manipulate thousands of elements in one work, a constant in all her work. She began her creative life as a loom weaver, explaining that for weavers "working with thousands of elements is not daunting; it's what we weavers work with every day" (interview). Her last public art commission at the Center for Jewish History in New York, entitled "Luminous Manuscript" (2004), also contained hundreds of thousands of elements.

Inspired by visions of cells seen under the microscope, "Lines of Sight" directly references microbiology and cell biology in its form and content. Viewers are encouraged to look closely at a small part of a gigantic whole, noting the beauty of a single cell. These cellular forms seem to float in plasma—a sea of clear glass dotted with tiny red beads and veins of text. The glass elements are, in fact, loosely contained inside the panels sandwiched between the inner and outer panes of glass. As in the body, every element in "Lines of Sight" is interdependent.

When constructing the panels Samuels needed to consider how to keep the glass elements from shifting when changing weather conditions (heat and cooling) affected the window panels, producing expansion and contraction. Samuels used a quilting metaphor to describe her patent pending process of holding all these loose elements together while working with the engineers: "Just as in quilting, when you have two pieces of fabric and cotton batting in between, every so often you need to put a stitch through all three layers," she explained when interviewed, and then asked, "What if we join the piece of glass every so often with adhesive?" The result was that the discs are held in place by the pressure of the glass and some occasional joiner elements acting like stitches that adhere to the glass.

The artist's hand—her manual labor—is evident throughout. The circular discs were hand-drawn by the artist translated into computer language and then cut by machine. The glass elements inside the panels were assembled by hand and all the text tiles were hand-engraved by the artist. Every panel

Figure 3
Diane Samuels, Detail of "Lines of Sight," looking through the lens in the window to the wide angle view of the exterior of the building. "Lines of Sight," Sidney E. Frank Hall for Life Sciences at Brown University.

Figure 4
Diane Samuels. One unit of "Lines of Sight" being fabricated by Samuels. "Lines of Sight," Sidney E. Frank Hall for Life Sciences at Brown University.

is unique. The artist treated each panel as a distinct entity like a tapestry or a collage, yet continued to think of the totality of the work. On occasion, a line of text or some other visual pattern continues from one panel into the next. These lines, like threads, are woven across and through the piece.

Samuels is a voracious reader and the idea for the inclusion of poetry into this public art work stemmed from her discovery of a poem by John Donne from 1572. "Poets throughout the centuries have written poems in response to advances in the life sciences: John Donne, for example, asked his readers, 'Know'st thou how blood, which to the heart doth floe, Doth from one ventricle to th' other go?' shortly after William Harvey first expounded his theory about the circulation of blood." The horizontal glass elements create new patterns in the biomorphic field of rounded glass—an insertion of the mental, verbal, human world into the biological, non-verbal one.

Samuels wanted to include other texts in the work so she expanded her search, asking the Brown University community—students, faculty, researchers, administration, staff, parents, alumni, friends—to email quotations from their favorite poetry or prose on the topic of "observing the world, discovery, perception, and looking closely. Quotations could be from poetry or prose with a 'poetic character' and the author could be anyone in any field: a writer, a scientist, the submitter." The texts span centuries and disciplines from the serious to the light-hearted. These horizontal glass pieces—chosen for their resemblance to microscope slides—were placed by the artist into the sea of disks to form arteries of visual movement. As viewers read, they move along and through the artwork, which becomes a roadway to others' thoughts and ideas about the world. The chosen texts talk about relationships between art and science, about experiencing the wonder of our world, being enlightened, and noticing when the invisible becomes visible.

The collection of texts gave Samuels the opportunity to discover writers she had never come across. All of this giving and taking, sharing and learning, during the process of the creation of the artwork, enriches the artist, who in turn enriches the public by translating what she has learned into the site-specific work.

Samuels also created a visual design for the outside glass panels of the bridge using two faint handprints sandblasted into the outside glass panels. The human hand has figured prominently in both Samuels' gallery and public art practice. She made handprints from participants in her projects in Buttenhausen, Germany ("Imprints and Artifacts," 1996) and for "Luminous Manuscript," at the Center for Jewish History in New York. These hands reaching across the Brown bridge span can be read as a metaphor for the bridge itself which allows for the connection between people and between the architectural spaces of the two buildings.

The hand was another way to symbolize the human presence in the work and to engage other members of the Brown community in the making of the piece. "I wanted to select an image for the exterior view that would relate to the life sciences. When I asked researchers if there was an image that wouldn't become outdated with advances in the field, they responded that the constant of life sciences was change. So I chose the image of a hand, used for centuries by Native Americans as

Figure 5
Diane Samuels. Detail view from inside of "Lines of Sight," looking through glass balls, disks, prisms, and engraved lines of poetry. "Lines of Sight" for the Sidney E. Frank Hall for Life Sciences at Brown University.

Exhibition Review
On Memory: Deborah Aschheim at the Mattress Factory

Exhibition Review
On Memory: Deborah Aschheim at the Mattress Factory

September 9, 2006 to January 28, 2007

On Memory, a new installation by Deborah Aschheim, opened on September 9, 2006, at Pittsburgh's Mattress Factory as one of four new works unveiled in the bi-annual *Factory Installed* series. Founded in 1977, the Mattress Factory grants residencies to selected artists, providing a space and as much as two months for the creation of a new body of work installed and exhibited at the museum. For Aschheim, the residency generated an ambitious, autobiographical investigation of the very process of recollection. *On Memory* occupies two gallery spaces. In the first room, a drawing that covers three walls maps Aschheim's family relations. Her memories of these characters are woven as neural networks in the adjoining room.

Since the early 1990s Aschheim has worked where the biological meets the technological. This location is constantly expanding as increasing technological abilities permit an understanding of ever smaller and previously undiscovered worlds. Aschheim uses her work to contend with the uncomfortable knowledge that systems and organisms invisible to us and often too minuscule to control determine the quality and length of our lives. The phenomenon of memory belongs to one such physically minute but functionally far-reaching realm.

On Memory, however, is anything but microscopic. Using floral grapes, medical tubing, pigmented polyurethane and diligence, Aschheim fabricated approximately 3,000 plastic nodes, the 3-inch dendrites and axons in her theoretical model of the neuronal structure of memory. Ten networks, woven with filament and thin clear rods, glow softly blue and purple, and reach from floor to ceiling throughout the dimly lit gallery. The colors are reminiscent of those used in brain imaging, yet the cool, clinical atmosphere of the installation is countered by the personal content at the center of each network. Aschheim collected home videos, which she describes as prosthetic memories, from the libraries of her father and grandfather. The form of each sculpture follows a map of Aschheim's recollections generated

REVIEWED BY LOTUS GRENIER

Figure 1
On Memory (installation view), 2006–7, plastic, light, video. Photo: Owen Smith

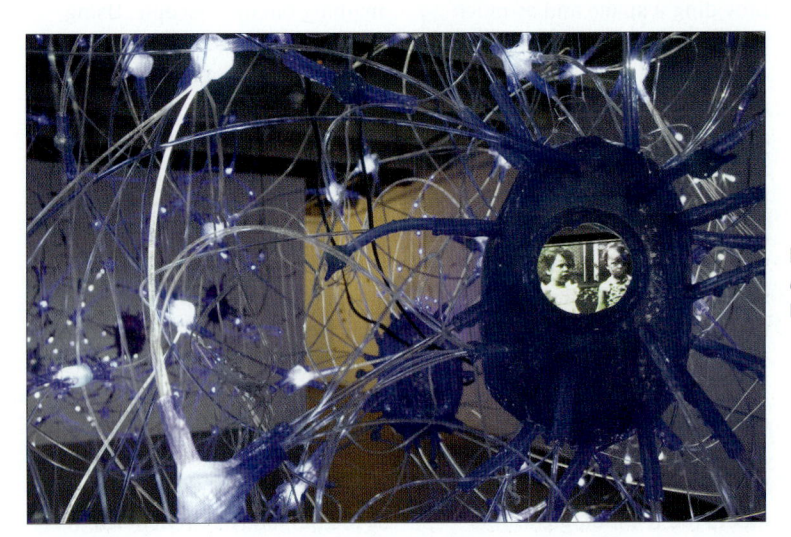

Figure 2
On Memory (detail), 2006–7, plastic, light, video. Photo: Owen Smith

by the film. These videos, like a physical prosthesis, support Aschheim's investigation of familial memory, a personal response to the Alzheimer's that is prevalent in her family. But because the video fragments are commonplace (a woman unlocking and getting into a car, children spinning circles playing ring-around-the-rosy, a family swimming in a lake), any viewer is offered a chance to follow his or her unique memories produced by the images. As the installation both portrays and stimulates the workings of memory, it is a literal weaving of a personal and schematic collapse.

Neural plasticity, the capacity of neural synapses to regenerate

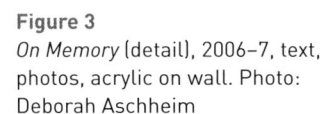

Figure 3
On Memory (detail), 2006–7, text, photos, acrylic on wall. Photo: Deborah Aschheim

and reroute, gives memory its characteristic fluidity, the frustrating but sometimes merciful ability to selectively or creatively remember. Yet memory is also generative of a life's narrative. Each time an incident is remembered, a new neural pathway is formed, which connects the recollection to the present moment and links it in such a way that the two events surface together upon subsequent remembering. Neural degenerative diseases such as Alzheimer's damage the connection and recall of events, destroying an individual's ability to recollect his story. The videos, photographs and family lore that remain are only abridged versions of a person that can be revisited and replayed, thereby becoming the material for new processes of creative interpretation. *On Memory*'s delicately woven neural networks physically depict this fragility of memory. The extensive and substantial web that connects both the generative fragments of family memorabilia and the thousands of ensuing recollections represented by the nodes, demonstrates the persistent, constructive work of memory over generations.

While the processes and functions of the brain are further untangled each year, the specific configuration of neural pathways remains in the territory of the imagined. It is exactly this limited scientific understanding that opens up the biological realm to art. Creative inquiry, whether in a gallery or in a laboratory, can generate ideas and representations that explore the indefinite. *On Memory* gives shape to the meeting of scientific modeling and experienced remembering.

Exhibition Review
Lia Cook: Re-Embodied

Exhibition Review
Lia Cook: Re-Embodied

Nancy Margolis Gallery, New York, March 2–April 22, 2006

I first encountered Lia Cook's work in her 2004 exhibition *Embedded Portraiture* at Perimeter Gallery in Chicago. Walking into the gallery, I found myself surrounded by large woven images—faces and cropped details of faces, mostly in black and white, some as large as a meter square. Though I recognized immediately the technical virtuosity of the work, it was something else that captivated me and that continues to fuel my curiosity about Cook's work.

Approaching one piece after the next, I became acutely aware of how the woven construction of the image frustrated my attempts to resolve that image. At a certain distance I could only see image, not thread. At another distance I could only see thread, not image. Standing at the precise threshold demarcating these two possible views of the work, and rocking first forward then back, I found that the resulting perceptual confusion released a particular affective response—something in proximity of grief or longing though not exactly either of those. Something that in a story would be evoked by the word *ago*. What was being enacted here went beyond a game of resolution and dissolution. I became convinced that this strong affective response, shared by many viewers of Cook's work, was triggered less by what was depicted than by something in the structure of the work itself. It is not that the face illustrates an emotion and so we feel, rather that in attempting to resolve the woven face we retrace a series of internal operations, and this retracing produces affect. An old record replayed by a new device.

Cook's show *Re-Embodied* in March 2006 at Nancy Margolis Gallery in New York presented me with an opportunity to re-experience the work and to attempt to tease apart how I understand her work to function. In doing so I want to consider the following: what is it about the inseparability of material and image in these works that makes them function differently than a painted, photographed, or printed image would? Is there value in considering the works as having a performative aspect and evaluating them as events rather than simply images or objects? With regard to this, are there craft-based conventions of presentation left unchallenged that interfere

REVIEWED BY JUDITH LEEMANN
Judith Leemann is an artist, educator, and writer living in Boston, Massachusetts. Currently teaching at Assumption College in Worcester, Massachusetts, and at the School of the Museum of Fine Arts, Boston, she is also Assistant Editor of the anthology *The Object of Labor: Art, Cloth, and Cultural Production* (School of the Art Institute of Chicago Press, 2007).

Textile, Volume 5, Issue 3, pp. 332–339
DOI: 10.2752/175183507X249503
Reprints available directly from the Publishers.
Photocopying permitted by licence only.
© 2007 Berg. Printed in the United Kingdom.

with the lay viewer's ability to see beyond the work's technical refinement and impressive investment of labor?

What does an infant see? For curious parents who want to know what their infant sees at birth, four weeks, eight weeks, the website www.tinyeyes.com allows one to submit a photograph, which is then processed according to an algorithm designed to alter the image so that it will look to an adult as the corresponding reality would look to the infant. Reproduced here is an image processed to show the development of sight from birth to six months to adulthood (Figure 1).

In Cook's earlier work, such as *Binary Traces: Blur* (2004; Figure 2), we are presented with large, unfocused faces peering out at us. It is telling that I am willing to call this a face, for it is in reality nothing more than two dark ovals where I know eyes to be, a dark line where I know a mouth to go, and a mottled curve that locates the other shadows on a round surface. My ability to resolve more than this is limited. Nothing I can do with my eyes will change the focus of what is presented. A perceptual limit is built into the work, for if I move closer as we know to do when trying to better see a thing, I lose the face entirely in the surface patterning of black and white threads. I am pushed back in my approach to the work. It holds me at a distance.

What distinguishes the approach to a woven image is that the dissolution of image into constituent parts upon approach is not the familiar dissolving into a field of printer's dots, photographic grain, or brushstrokes, but is rather the resolving and recognition of another dimensional object— thread. The material has body; the image is re-embodied. One does not lose sight of the work nor lose oneself in the work, but is, rather, tracked along a narrative in which one sees, sways momentarily at a threshold, and then sees again. One does not fall into the work, but is pushed back again by the patterning at this second, smaller scale. I would argue that what makes Cook's work so powerful and so *not* limited to the technical, is this performative aspect of the work—the way in which it scripts a particular perceptual encounter.

In recent works, such as *In the Maze* (2005; Figure 3), that encounter is complicated by superimposing the micro-pattern of threads over the image as a whole.

Figure 1
Simulation of what the infant sees at a distance of 36 in. at birth, four weeks, eight weeks, three months, six months, and as an adult. Photograph of performer Mark Jeffery (www.tinyeyes.com).

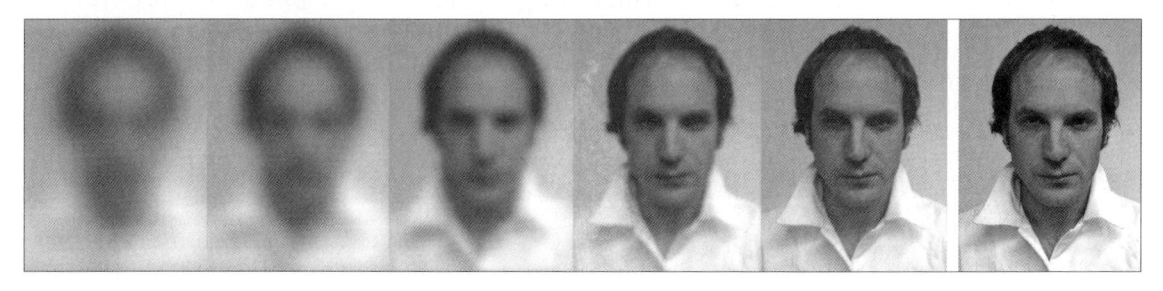

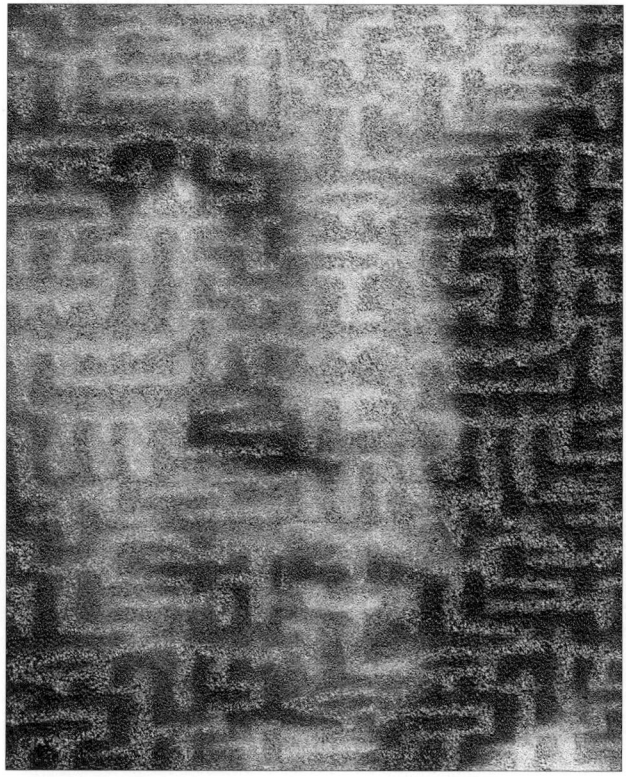

Figure 2
Lia Cook, *Binary Traces: Blur*, 2004, 56 in. × 50 in. cotton, woven.

Figure 3
Lia Cook, *In the Maze*, 2005, 66 in. × 53 in., cotton, woven.

With the older works, standing back after seeing the cloth up close, I had to mentally add my memory of the detail to my current seeing of the whole. Now though, the micro-pattern is reinscribed into the cloth—the after-image made material, guaranteed recognition. The perceptual task of the viewer now includes the labor of seeing through an interference pattern to find that thing our eyes spend so much of their time seeking out—the face. Enfolded within the seeing of the distant view is the necessary subtraction of interfering information. Perhaps the equation of that labor looks something like this: distant view of face (what is seen minus the interfering micro-pattern) plus close-up view of the substance of the piece (micro-pattern of threads).

Doubling abounds. Recursive circles loop and repeat. Thresholds are crossed and recrossed.

This tight cycle of self-reference echoes and makes sense of works that in their apparent simplicity might at first appear out of keeping with the rest of the exhibition. In these works, *Embedded Digits* (2004; Figure 4) and *Material Digits* (2005; Figure 5), we see hands touching each other, being brought to touch lips, cheeks. Among those who study nonverbal communication, self-touching refers to those gestures, apparently without purpose, in which the body reaches back for itself—rubbing the chin, squeezing the hands together, touching the fingers to the lips. Once thought to be indicators of negative affect—ways of displacing unwanted emotion, they are now also considered to play a role in the production and processing of information. One recent study, for example, found increased self-touching behavior as subjects were asked to recall a list of words given

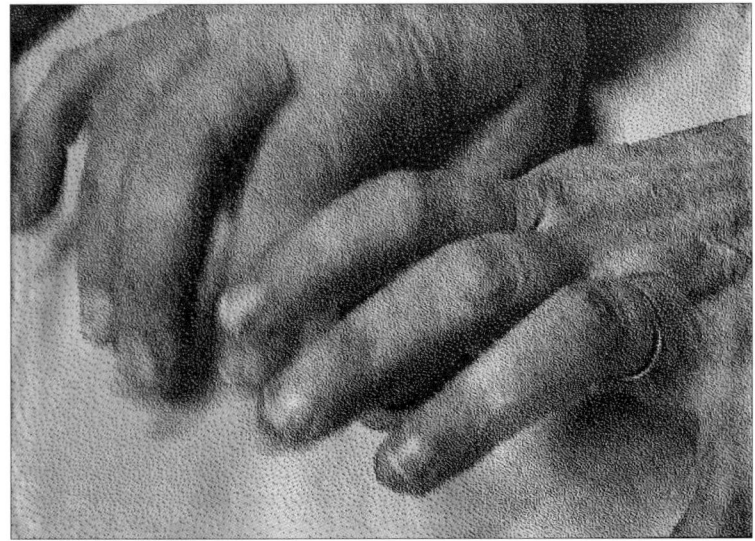

Figure 4
Lia Cook, *Embedded Digits*, 2004, 37 in. × 50 in., cotton, woven.

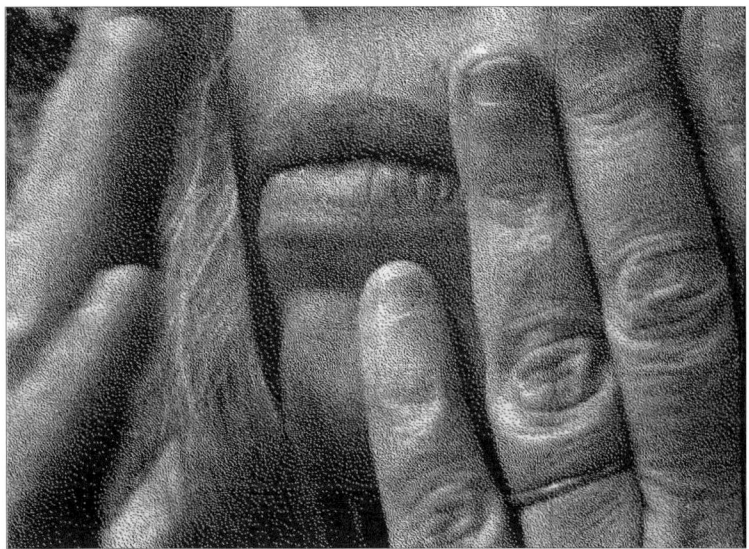

Figure 5
Lia Cook, *Material Digits*, 2005, 40 in. × 52 in., cotton, woven.

to them two weeks prior. We know these gestures, each have our own vocabulary, bringing together, reassuring, reinscribing a self. These gestures are made at times of uncertainty, in moments of loss, need—the sudden and involuntary gesture of bringing one's hands over one's mouth. In the way Cook constructs her work, as in our own use of such gestures, we see the productive capacity of circling back on oneself.

That the works are woven and not painted, printed, or embroidered is significant, but this crucial difference is downplayed by how the works are presented. For the viewer who understands weaving and how works like these are constructed, these are not flat frontal images. We know they have a back, know that they are dimensional artifacts of the process of threads lifting and crossing. The back of such a double cloth will by necessity hold the negative image of the front, and in the richness of Cook's play among binaries—black and white, up and down, here and gone, it comes as a loss to encounter only front. Neatly sewn along the edges, the work seems at this final moment to submit to the conventions of craft and the presentation of high-end textile work. What would happen if the raw backside were offered?

Watching and listening to gallery visitors, there was a well-deserved attention to the intricacy and technical virtuosity of these works. Cook's work certainly merits recognition of its highly sophisticated craft, but I worry that this technical "wow factor" is also an endpoint for many viewers who do not share the insider's knowledge of what kind of object is before them. With her evident understanding of how to build in constructive interferences, might there be a way for Cook to interfere with this tendency—to disturb the edges of the viewing experience itself?

The perceptual script Cook embeds in her works is not an optional way to look at the work, it is the sequence of what one *does* do in order to see the work. The sequence of looking and looking again follows from the way in which Cook has constructed these works. And so it is fair to consider this embedded script an integral part of the structure of the work. Physically the works are woven double-cloths of black and white cotton threads. But in a performative sense they are scores for a certain sequence and timing of perceptual additions and subtractions operating inside the viewer.

I want to speculate that the internal operations required to see Cook's work are enough like those of the infant first learning to see—looking out, subtracting elongated, branched projections and nodules to create interleaved mappings, which oscillate between registering as an image of neuron activity or ganglia, MRI films of the soft tissue workings of the human body, or anatomical diagrams and models of instruction (Figure 1). In *Transmitter I* (Figure 2), a spillage of vellum florets holding pools of dried ink is pierced by networks of tubes, wire, and acrylic rods that project out from the wall to create a connective architecture that suggests a hushed interior communication highway of cells, neurons, and dendrites or perhaps an entire living organism. The inspired forms and fabricated views into the interior workings of cells and their connective relationships mirror the pulse of activity at work in our own bodies. The title, *Mars under My Skin* (Figure 3), reveals the mystery the artist shares with members of her audience in (not) knowing the exact process and functioning of her own body, or how bodily sensations are precisely generated and registered. Like the function of individual cells, our bodies move through the space we inhabit, vulnerable to invasion, sensitive to structural damage, susceptible to environmental imbalance, yet capable of resilience and performing incredibly complex tasks.

The title piece, *Sensory Jetty* (Figure 4), combines the formal characteristics and differences of these possible life forms. Individualized shapes are suspended over and submerged within watery planes of white vellum and blue vinyl to offer an imagined view into an entire ecological system. The acrylic rods used in *Sensory Jetty* pass through the wall that supports it. This wall

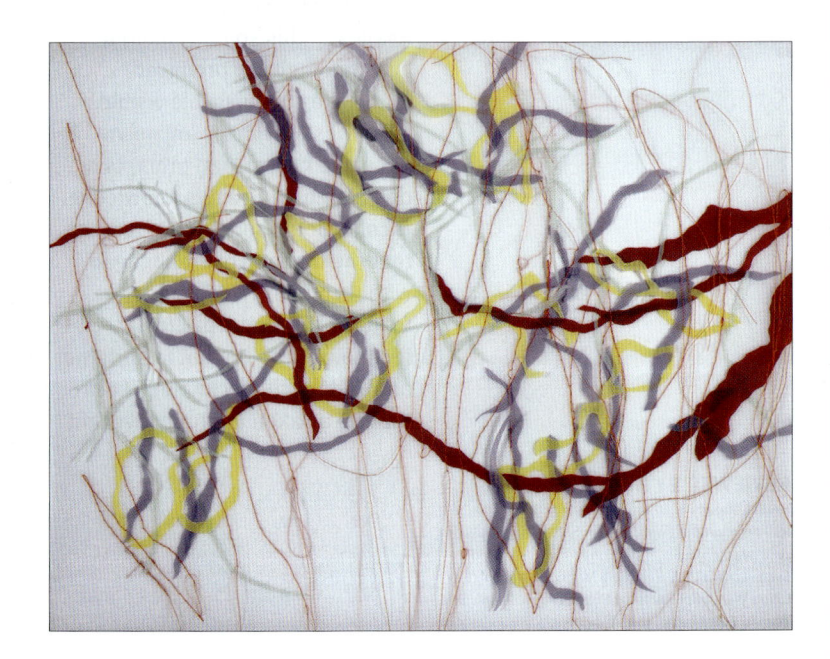

Figure 1
Synapse, 2006, vellum and thread, 11 in. × 14 in. (28 cm × 36 cm).

Exhibition Review

Figure 2
Transmitter I, 2007, ink on vellum, vinyl, wire, thread, and rubber, 21 in. × 15 in. × 15 in. (53 cm × 38 cm × 38 cm).

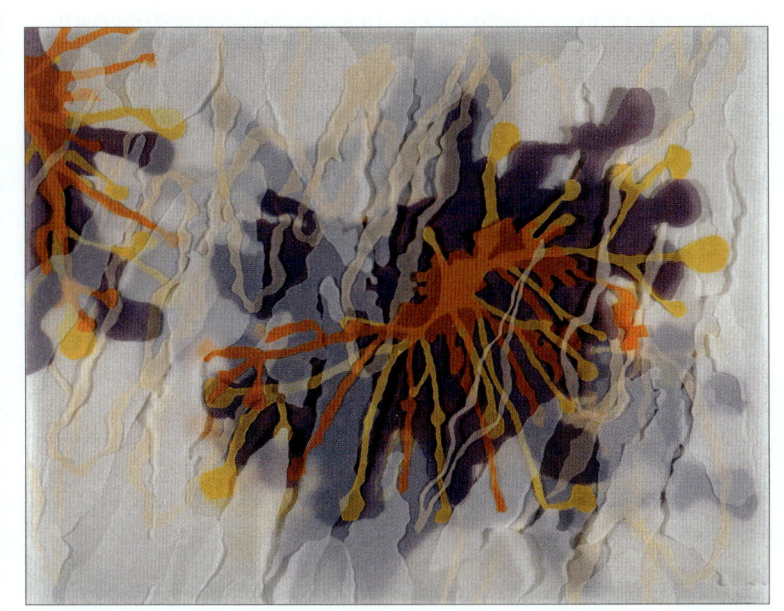

Figure 3
Mars under My Skin, 2006, vellum, 11 in. × 14 in. (28 cm × 36 cm).

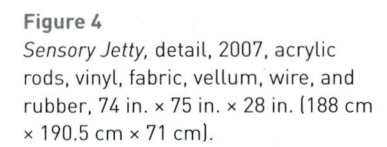

Figure 4
Sensory Jetty, detail, 2007, acrylic rods, vinyl, fabric, vellum, wire, and rubber, 74 in. × 75 in. × 28 in. (188 cm × 190.5 cm × 71 cm).

sits two feet in from, and parallel to, the wall that marks the exterior of the building. A window permits a view from the street below into the gallery and to the backside of *Sensory Jetty*. Daylight, passing through this window, flows across and passes through the acrylic rods to illuminate their tips on the other side. The tips create bright dots of neon green and yellow that echo light-emitting diodes (LEDs). Electrical impulses of the life actively inhabiting this world are made visible and the concept of the wall is changed from solid partition to "membrane."[2] At night the piece is artificially lit from behind, which serves to maintain the LED effect. Inside the gallery, unless one ventures around to the two-foot space between the partition and window for a closer look, the permeability of the wall, the view from the street, and the exact source of the LED-like illumination carry on unnoticed.

Like the exhibition's title piece, *Seeping In* (see Figure 5) includes the wall and gallery space in the interplay of seen and unseen, known and unknown. Safe-T-Gallery is accessed via an interior corridor. An interior window sits to the left of the gallery door. Positioned in front of this window, shadows cast onto a sheet of vellum create an X-ray-like image when viewed from the corridor. This window-become-X-ray both exposes and obscures *Seeping In*. The X-ray-like image also prevents a visitor from seeing into the gallery to view other works in the exhibition.

Once inside the gallery, one learns that a piece of silk is the mass that casts the shadow on the other side. The cut and stitched fragment is suspended gracefully yet eerily on a one-inch grid of woven nylon thread strung across a large acrylic frame. The grid sits above and in front of a large sheet of vellum. The spaces between these layered parts subtly yet radically disrupt the typical visual and scientific process used to

Figure 5
Seeping In, detail, 2004, silk fabric, hand-dyed embroidery thread, nylon thread, Plexiglas, and vellum, 30 in. × 24 in. × 4 in. (76 cm × 61 cm × 10 cm).

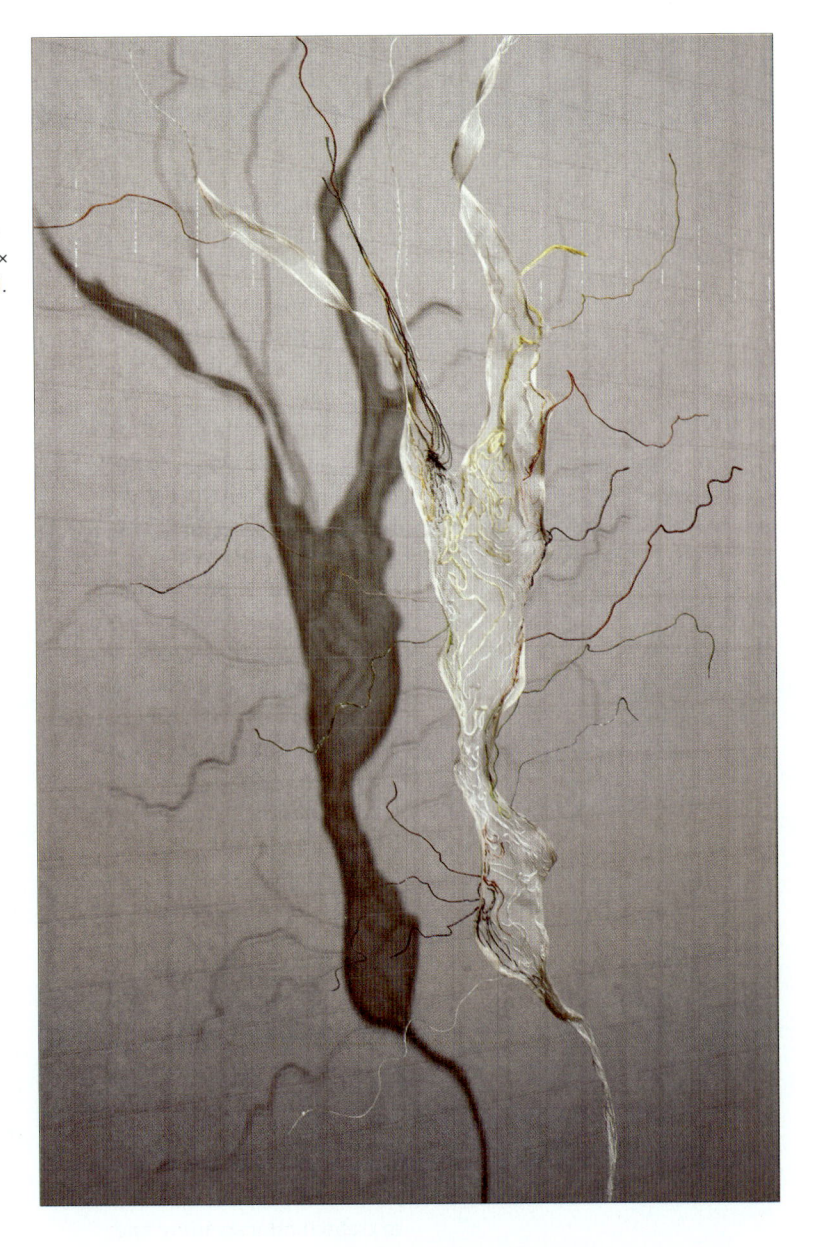

explore this skin, bacteria, virus, or tissue (remove it from its source, place it in controlled conditions, restrict its movement, and subject the observations made to a set framework of investigation) and propose a yet-to-be-determined method of inquiry.

Points of view, trains of thought, and mental outlooks create both virtual and physical forms, which in turn create frameworks for social interaction (Bourriaud 2002[1998]: 58). Cultural convention, a virtual form, tells us our bodies are separate from the bodies of others.

Neuhaus's inexact yet repeated attempt at replicating cellular, somatic forms unlocks this cultural convention. The term "body" and the accepted understanding of cutting and connection are opened, and give way to new possibilities for subjectivity.

In *Sensory Jetty*, Neuhaus has seized the flow of art inherent in Eva Hesse's work not by imitation or appropriation of the corporeal, but by extension of the virtual. To behold Hesse's sculptural work is to teeter limitlessly at the fissure of the psyche (the virtual space of the body and subjectivity) and the corporeal body itself. This internal emotional dissonance was captured in Hesse's forms to create an intimate place for the viewer in relation to the industrial dominance of minimalist art. Neuhaus releases this internal teetering into and onto the spaces of the multiple bodies made (partially) known by technology through forms that model cohabitation and coexistence for the human body with other bodies at the site where technology meets life (the microscope, the laboratory, the MRI, the surgical table or Petri dish).

As a body of work, *Sensory Jetty* propels and awakens us to the limitless possibility of understanding "bodies" as a collection of observable and invisible, knowable and secretive, independent worlds of life. These bodies pulse and exchange information in continuous connection, of which we are part, and from which we attempt to create understanding and relationship. Rather than a utopian vision offered by a specialist, Neuhaus's engagement with the inter-effects of technology and biology is an enchanted imaginary proposition open to negotiation and participation. Her forms carry us to a threshold of sensation and perception that an ethical exploration of bodies demands and continuously brings. This is a virtual space extracted from the power of technology, and the flow of life, organized with an aesthetic sensibility "allowing viewers to imagine what is under the surface and on the skin, to see inside and be within."[3]

Notes

1. Artist's statement printed for the exhibition made available to the author courtesy of Safe-T-Gallery.
2. Author's interview with the artist, March 23, 2007.
3. Artist's statement.

References

Bourriaud, Nicolas. 2002[1998]. *Relational Aesthetics*. Trans. Simon Pleasance and Fronza Woods with Mattieu Copeland. Dijon: Les presses du réel.

Deleuze, Gilles and Félix Guattari. 1987. *A Thousand Plateaus: Capitalism and Schizophrenia*. Trans. Brian Massumi. Minneapolis, MN: University of Minnesota Press.

Exhibition Review
Radical Lace and Subversive Knitting

Exhibition Review
Radical Lace and Subversive Knitting

Museum of Arts and Design, New York, January 25–June 17, 2007

The *Radical Lace and Subversive Knitting* exhibition at the Museum of Arts and Design in New York brings together works by twenty-seven artists who have expanded knitting and lace out of the realm of the domestic and the feminine, into a more public domain. The opening text panel offers broad definitions of knitting and lace, in keeping with the great variety of processes used to create the works in the exhibition. Knitting is defined as work involving one continuous strand, while lace indicates the presence of transparency. These reductive definitions greatly expand the parameters of both knitting and lace, ushering in a survey of contemporary fiber art from eleven different countries.

The museum's Chief Curator David Revere McFadden has conceived the exhibition around six themes: Corporeal Constructions, Matters of Scale, Light Constructions, Interconnections, Creative Deconstructions, and The Beauty of Complexity. One could imagine other categories that would be equally useful since there are multiple aspects that link various works to each other, including where they fall along the range from handmade to technologically produced. However, the works from each thematic group are intermixed throughout the exhibition. This leaves the viewer to make his or her own connections, but also confuses the viewer as to how the connections are made.

The Museum of Arts and Design has turned over the majority of their three-floor exhibition space to this show, which is sufficient for the forty works on view. Mesh screens have been placed between some of the works, rather than solid wall partitions, which helps keep the space open even while it affords individual works their own niche. The screens also fit in well with the work in the exhibition, which ranges from large-scale installations to miniatures.

Two of the artists knit clothing from paper. Erna Van Sambeek's *Bodywarmers for a Poor Family* includes scarves, socks, slippers,

REVIEWED BY JULIE REISS
Julie H. Reiss is an associate professor in the graduate program at Christie's Education, New York. She received her PhD in art history from the Graduate Center of the City University of New York. In addition to teaching, Reiss has held curatorial positions at the Guggenheim Museum and the Jewish Museum. She is the author of *From Margin to Center: The Spaces of Installation Art* (MIT Press, 1999). Reiss recently published "Sounds Affect: The Auditory Experience in Installation Art," in *Klangkunst – Sonambiente 2006* (Akademie der Künste, 2006). She has lectured extensively at museums in New York including the Museum of Modern Art and the Metropolitan.

Textile, Volume 5, Issue 3, pp. 348–355
DOI: 10.2752/175183507X249521
Reprints available directly from the Publishers.
Photocopying permitted by licence only.
© 2007 Berg. Printed in the United Kingdom.

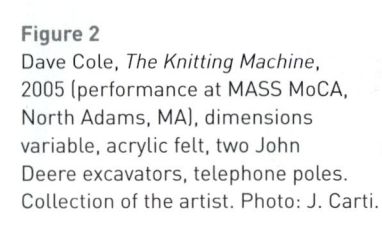

Figure 2
Dave Cole, *The Knitting Machine*, 2005 (performance at MASS MoCA, North Adams, MA), dimensions variable, acrylic felt, two John Deere excavators, telephone poles. Collection of the artist. Photo: J. Carti.

Figure 3
Edward Mayer, *Drawing In*, 2006 (installation view at Schick Gallery, Skidmore College, Saratoga Springs, New York), dimensions variable, steel shelving, found objects, vinyl tape, wood, plastic zip ties. Collection of the artists; courtesy Zabriskie Gallery, New York. Photo: Edward Mayer.

Club, the work is colorful and transparent. The hand-knotting technique Echelman employed is based on techniques used to create Indian fishing nets, but here the nylon net is formed into the shape of a mushroom cloud. The colors in the piece are determined by the colors of the flags of the countries known to have detonated nuclear weapons. The form is deceptively light and playful, swirled in red, green, blue, white, and yellow stripes.

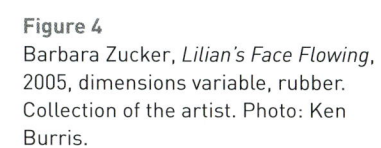

Figure 4
Barbara Zucker, *Lilian's Face Flowing*, 2005, dimensions variable, rubber. Collection of the artist. Photo: Ken Burris.

A work that successfully brings handwork into the political arena is an interactive installation by Sabrina Gschwandtner titled *Wartime Knitting Circle*. Gschwandtner found photographic documentation of times throughout history in which knitting was put to use during wartime. Through a service that creates portrait blankets from photos, she had the photographs transferred into black and white acrylic knit blankets. The moments depicted on the blankets range from the Volunteers for the Ontario Voice of Knitting making camouflage clothes for the Vietnamese, to a recent image of the Daughters of the American Revolution knitting squares for blankets for US soldiers in Iraq and Afghanistan. The blankets hang around a table strewn with wool, needles, and patterns for several items to which the knitting visitor can contribute, depending on one's level of skill. I added a few rows to a nine-inch square that will join other squares eventually and become an afghan blanket that will be sent to Afghanistan. One could also work on a helmet liner. The current projects link the viewer/participant to the history of knitting during wartime. While I was knitting, other visitors to the exhibition came over and joined me. It was oddly relaxing to sit in a museum in midtown Manhattan and knit. It was also an effective reminder of the world outside the museum.

Overall, the exhibition succeeds on several levels. While many of the works do grab our attention visually, an understanding of the process is an important part of what makes them interesting, and the exhibition rewards patient perusal of the texts in order to understand the processes involved. At its core, the exhibition focused on the performative aspects, the process of making the work and physically experiencing the materials. The emphasis on the performative and the social and political aspects of handcrafts, clearly connect the work to installation and performance post-1960. As a result some of the works would be equally at home in a group exhibition of contemporary art, but not all of the works cross over, and this is an interesting issue to ponder as one walks through. Above all, the exhibition is timely, coming as it does at a point where there is increasing dialogue about craft and its radical nature. Next year at the College Art Association's annual conference, a session titled "Gestures of Resistance: Craft, Performance and the Politics of Slowness" will be presented, postulating "a theory of handcraft as performative: active, public and affective, rather than passive, private and obsessive."[1] *Radical Lace and Subversive Knitting* takes its place in this dialog.

Note

1. Shannon Stratton and Judith Leeman, "2008 Call for Participation," *College Art Association* 2007: 20.

Book Reviews

Art Textiles of the World: Scandinavia
Matthew Koumis

The Sculpture of Ruth Asawa: Contours in the Air
Daniell Cornell

Reinventing Textiles:
Volume 1: Tradition and Innovation
Sue Rowley
Volume 2: Gender and Identity
Janis Jefferies
Volume 3: Postcolonialism and Creativity
Paul Sharrad and Anne Collett

Findings: The Material Culture of Needlework and Sewing
Mary C. Beaudry

Book Review

***Art Textiles of the World: Scandinavia* (Volume 2), Matthew Koumis (ed.) (Brighton: Telos Art Publishing, 2005)**

The *Art Textiles of the World* series currently offers eleven publications on seven different countries, and besides giving a wonderful opportunity to see a concentration of textile art from a particular country it allows scrutiny of information other than the work itself. The series, as it grows, increasingly allows opportunity to see if different preoccupations and approaches from each nation are detectable. It is also possible to see the network of global connections in textile art through the lists of exhibitions the contributors have taken part in, in this volume predominantly throughout mainland Europe, with occasional links with Japan, the UK, USA, and Australia. From the evidence of grants and awards given in the CV, some, unbelievably, for fifteen years, it would seem that Scandinavian countries provide a good structure of financial support for artists and craftspeople.

In each volume, the contributors, here from Iceland, Norway, Finland, Denmark, and Sweden, each have ten pages of images of work, one of themselves, text, and a brief résumé. The work, which is highly professional and well photographed, is considered alongside non-theoretical, sometimes anecdotal, testimonies from the artists. These accounts of the process of developing ideas and the direct experience of material curiosity and knowledge are sincere and personally expressed. I find the photographs of the contributors shift attention away from the work to the personality of the maker and it is irritating when occasionally a work is discussed in the text but is not illustrated.

Most of the work is relatively large-scale, wall-based work. It includes: technical virtuosity such as the work of Ingunn Skogholt and Agneta Hobin, whose aesthetics are rooted in craft and design traditions and where nature, color, and light are cited as the driving forces; the open-ended nature of Monica Nilsson's interdisciplinary installations; Silja Puranen's questioning of the perceptions and control of ideal and actual body shape and image; and the powerful layering of textile upon textile of Bente Saetrang. There are references to traditional textile training, domesticity, design, and an appreciation of ways in which these contribute to the

REVIEWED BY
CAROLINE BROADHEAD

continuity of textile practice, an acknowledgment of the capacity of textiles to hold memory and history and to associate with age and gender, as well as a recognition of the commitment of time textiles often demands.

The book is easily navigated, well laid out, and has simple and clear graphics. The selection of contributors is the personal choice of editor and founder of Telos Art Publishing, Matthew Koumis, and he does not justify or comment apart from a brief and general sentence in the opening of his introduction. Letting the work speak for itself is an acceptable strategy. However, the introduction develops into an appeal for textile art to be elevated to equal status with mainstream art. His is an outside-looking-in attitude, textiles are "in the ghetto," he is dismayed by textile art being "hung in the Crafts Museums, in between sixties pots and eighties earrings." This is an extremely patronizing view of both practitioners and the audiences of craft museums. He quotes a survey of one hundred people conducted outside the Tate Modern who were shown pictures of textile art and asked to comment on whether they considered it to be equal, better or worse than work displayed the Tate Modern. This is a laughably inadequate survey, inconclusive and superficial. It does not do the series justice. It might have served his purpose better to have commissioned an essay to introduce and contextualize this work in more depth.

Despite this, Koumis is to be applauded for his sustained involvement in promoting and celebrating textile art. By publishing these books, he is strengthening and building the area of art textiles and focusing and further linking a global network. It is a very positive thing to do.

Book Review

***The Sculpture of Ruth Asawa: Contours in the Air.* Daniell Cornell (ed.) (San Francisco, London: University of California Press, 2006)**

There is a buoyant optimism about Ruth Asawa, her belief that "sculpture is like farming, if you just keep at it you can get quite a lot done" reflects the virtues of honest toil and lots of backbreaking hard work. *The Sculpture of Ruth Asawa: Contours in the Air* provides considerable and useful detail on her background, training, working processes, and community involvement. The style of the introduction and most of the eight essays is largely laudatory and inclined to the homily. With the exception of Emily K. Doman Jennings' essay the approaches are biographical rather than providing critical context. The ninth contribution to the publication is an interview with the artist and her husband Albert Lanier, conducted in 2002 by Paul J. Karlstrom. From this interview it is interesting to catch a flavor of the woman herself. For example, how she positions herself within the Modernist tradition: "I was experimenting before anything was called modern, at that time just experimenting." Or the importance of materials within her work: "We were so poor that we were taking materials that were around us and using leaves and rocks and things that were natural."

The editor Daniell Cornell has divided the catalog into three sections of essays categorized as: personal narrative, contribution to modern art, arts education and the community. In effect, this produces three interrelated strands: formative influences, particularly the habits of hard work, the immediate and continuing influence of Black Mountain College in determining her working practice, and Asawa's ethnicity as a Japanese American—an important factor in post-World War Two America. The essays present the reader with a coherent narrative of Asawa's life and creative development—strong on biographical detail but largely lacking in critical appraisal.

Families of poor farmers know how it is to respond to the seasons, packing fruit, gathering vegetables in the heat and dust, using and reusing all available materials. Asawa's Japanese parents needed seven children to cope with the demands of a slowly expanding area of reluctantly productive land in Norwalk, CA. Many of the skills

REVIEWED BY LESLEY MILLAR

learned during this time reemerged later in Asawa's work. Saturday off for all the children was spent in Japanese school maintaining Japanese traditions. Calligraphy and the understanding of how the spaces between the marks were as important as the strokes made by the brush underpinned her later development as an artist. Curiously, the war provided Asawa with her first opportunity to hear artist's discussions and watch them working whilst she was interned at Santa Anita, CA, and later at Rohwer Relocation Center in Arkansas. The war also offered the possibility for training as a teacher, which Asawa took up. However, she never fully qualified because, as a Japanese, as she was unable to undertake probationary work as a teacher.

In 1945, Asawa traveled to Mexico with her sister. In Mexico City she observed the techniques women used to make crocheted baskets from wire; this was to become a formative influence in her work. She joined the newly formed art school La Escuela Nacionale de Pintura y Escultura La Esmerelda and also took an art class at the Universidad de Mexico taught by the furniture designer Clara Porset. It was this teacher who recommended that she go to Black Mountain College, reinforcing Asawa's earlier interest in the College.

Mary Emma Harris's meticulously researched essay describes Asawa's experience of Black Mountain College. Arriving at Black Mountain College was bewildering in many ways for her. She was not used to making decisions, or the freedom to determine her own course structure. Initially she had wished to study weaving with Anni Albers, but Albers, who was leaving for a sabbatical, felt there was insufficient time and advised her to take Josef Albers design course. This painting, drawing, and color course suited Asawa's reluctance to make decisions. The course was prescriptive, modeled on severely sequential exercises, with judgments restricted to the efficacy of visual language skills as exemplified by Josef Albers: "you leave your feelings to your spare time." For Asawa this was perfect, and her pages of visual notes and exercises, faithfully reproduced within the book, show a remarkable ability to use Bauhaus training productively. The balance of "blue skies thought" from John Cage, Buckminster Fuller, and a range of professional artists including Robert Rauschenberg and Willem de Kooning introduced her to the discipline of critically appraising her own work.

Asawa's intention was to become a painter, but the close relationship of disciplines and the lack of hierarchy at Black Mountain College between all "making" drew her towards three-dimensional studies and a transparent, linear approach to sculpture. Her work then, and subsequently, emphasized the essential Bauhaus concern with the interrelationship between material process and form. The fascination that Josef Albers, Mark Tobey, Cage and Merce Cunningham had for Asian philosophy provided the route for Asawa's ethnicity to inform her work. Asawa uses a cellular technique, which is both repetitive and organic. Japanese artists refer to this as a response to nature, which does not mean the depiction of nature, more the embodiment of the forces of nature. Much of this can be seen in the work of contemporary Japanese textile artist Machiko Agano, which although equally dependent on a basic knitted form, is much less circumscribed.

In her essay "Critiquing the Critique: Ruth Asawa's Early Reception," Emily K. Doman Jennings describes how the 1950s and early 1960s preoccupation with compartmentalization clearly defines Asawa's predicament. Asawa was categorized by her ethnicity (Japanese American was considered acceptable as a "conquered" wife), her sex ("housewife" and "mother of six children"), and the proximity of her sculpture to craft (textile) techniques. Crafts at the time carried connotations of conservatism and resistance to change. Clement Greenberg, writing in 1956, saw much American sculpture as being fashioned in ways that had its roots in organic form, resulting in "superior forms of garden statuary." Greenberg considered this form of American sculpture as *objets d'art* as opposed to David Smith's "Fine Art Sculpture." In this kind of comparison Asawa's Looped Wire works lack the muscular maleness of welded steel, the technical relationship of her work to the female knitting and knotting placed the work outside the accepted cannon. The obsessive labeling of the 1950s confined/defined Asawa by her ethnicity and gender.

This publication is a beautifully illustrated story of a life well lived against a background of model student, wife, mother, artist, local activist, including informative reproductions from the Black Mountain course demonstrating Asawa's visual fluency. There are many atmospheric photographs of the harmonious development of house and children and a life lived fully in the community, contributing resourcefully to the creative and imaginative requirements of local elementary schoolchildren. The critical substantiation of Asawa's position as a sculptor in this collection of essays is insufficiently robust however. There is a glimpse of the context in which work was seen and made and its reception but no more than a glimpse.

Book Review

Reinventing Textiles: Volume 1: *Tradition and Innovation*, Sue Rowley (ed.) (Brighton: Telos Art Publishing, 1999, reprinted 2004); Volume 2: *Gender and Identity*, Janis Jefferies (ed.) (Brighton: Telos Art Publishing, 2001); Volume 3: *Postcolonialism and Creativity*, Paul Sharrad and Anne Collett (eds) (Brighton: Telos Art Publishing, 2004)

The textile art community already had reason to be grateful to Matthew Koumis of Telos Publishing for the useful, beautifully produced, and popular *Art Textiles of the World* series and for the growing *Portfolio* series on individual makers. Though more modest in appearance, the three volumes of the *Reinventing Textiles* series, published over the last seven years, may arguably be the most important contribution to serious discussions of textile art. The 2004 reprinting of the first volume testifies to a widespread positive response from makers, scholars, and students.

Though each volume focuses on a separate set of issues in textile practice and research, there is throughout a welcome and wide-ranging combination of the formal and the informal, with personal accounts of making complementing the more challenging research accounts. In the first volume, *Tradition and Innovation*, editor Sue Rowley establishes the wide international view that marks the whole series, with contributions from Australia, India, the UK, USA, Hong Kong, Spain and Poland. Some of the essays, like Diana Wood Conroy's exploration of parallels between Australian weaving and ancient artefacts from Cyprus, suggest novel ways of looking at interrelationships across the spaces of time as well as geography. Concern with interlocking cultural and sociopolitical dimensions of practice is a recurrent theme. The editor's eighteen-page overview, "Craft, Creativity and Critical Practice," is far more than an introduction. It explores, in a substantially theorized but accessible way, the interrelationships informing making and serious thinking about current practice. There is an anthropological flavor to some of the discussions, looking at how the objects function within specific contexts while acknowledging the complexity of those contexts when they become ingredients in aesthetic judgments. Though the range of contributions in the volume is richly diverse, this essay alone seems worth the price of the volume.

REVIEWED BY
JUDITH DUFFEY HARDING

The second volume, *Gender and Identity*, edited by Janis Jefferies, also gathers a diverse international collection of views on the cultural and political issues that have played key roles in work of the last decade. The national contexts represented are fewer, and more heavily weighted to Europe and North America, though Australia, Israel, and South Korea are represented. Like the first volume, there is a mix of the theoretical and first-person accounts of the experience of making and the meanings that evolve from that tactile practice, Canadian Peter Hobbs, for example, explores the metaphoric potential for "the queer ear" of the mechanics of the sewing machine, a device associated with domestic tradition. He sees the relationship of machine and operator as "something of a machine–human hybrid or automaton," hinting at the transition to cyborg that our newest "machine," the computer, offers.

This account of a solitary dialogue between maker and machine is echoed in Kay Lawrence and Lindsay Obermeyer's collaborative reflections over distance. Their exchanges chart the thinking processes of two makers as they each struggle to give tangible form to the notion of reciprocity in relationships. This concern with the role of dialogue in seeing making as a socially situated practice marks many of the contributions here. The inclusion of Sarat Maharaj's 1992 essay "Textile Art: Who Are You?," describing his grandmother's recycling of parachute silk, "at once sacred cloth and object of warfare, life-saving and death-dealing engine," establishes a theme that runs through the volume, of the power of personal association with the potential of textile that is worn and used, becoming both the physical stuff and the metaphorical thread of lives and connections.

Similar concerns inform the third volume, *Postcolonialism and Creativity*, edited by Paul Sharrad and Anne Collett. Though equally international in scope, this volume has a more unified feel as a result of its emergence as a collection of papers and presentations given at the "Fabrications of the Postcolonial: Textiles, Texts and Trade" conference in 2002 at the University of Wollongong, Australia. The aim of "bringing together creative practice and scholarly analysis" had the effect of charting "attempts to cross between 'creative arts' scholarship and postcolonial studies as worked through literatures." More than the previous volumes in this series, this group seems to focus on the circumstances surrounding the specific materials and objects of making more than processes. A quick scan through the titles gives a flavor; "shawl, underwear, buckskin, appliqué, currency cloth, silk-screen, weaving." Again, these papers are a refreshing combination of the very personal accounts of process, and the more theorized considerations of the effects of national identity and migration. Another interesting difference, perhaps resulting from the editors' professional starting points in literature, is the inclusion of two papers using Salmon Rushdie's work as a starting point.

As a whole, these three volumes represent a rich contribution to recent and current understanding of the debates around textile practice. They bridge a gap between discussions of individual makers' approaches and the larger theoretical and cultural issues of identity and gender that have become the staple of current textile discussions. The inclusion of a generous center section of color photographs is supported by black and white photographs throughout the volume. The impression reverses that of much textile publication, which prioritizes large-scale detailed photographs of work with minimal descriptive text. In this series, the small format unashamedly prioritizes the text but acknowledges the need for visual evidence to discuss the visual; the impression is of an academic journal with images rather than a visual book with "accompanying" text.

We can hope that future volumes will continue to develop this project. An intriguing note on Volume 2 suggests that the next volume was intended to be a collection on the politics of curatorship. Other potential territories for future investigation and collection spring to mind, for instance, the notions of "vernacular craft" that characterize textile communities outside the art school culture, contrasting subcultures within some areas of textiles like quilting, the positioning of makers who anonymously fabricate works for "fine artists" who work in textiles, or the fascinating recent developments in digital approaches to making. We will certainly watch this space with interest.

Book Review

Findings: The Material Culture of Needlework and Sewing,
Mary C. Beaudry (New Haven, CT, and London: Yale University Press, 2006)

A privy at the back of a mid-nineteenth-century brothel in New York may be an unusual starting point for a book review in this journal. But *Findings* is a deliberately inclusive book, and the privy's recent excavation yielded an assortment of tools for fancy needlework and lace-making that lent themselves well to Mary C. Beaudry's investigation. She musters various interpretations of the finds from the privy, including the suggestion that their owner occupied herself with mending and embroidery whilst she waited for clients, and that they served in an attempt to project luxury and respectability "in the midst of squalor." Mary Beaudry herself suggests the tools may have served "as an alternative income strategy" for the prostitute. Whatever the reading of them, it is clear that the prostitute's needlework tools remain, on paper at least (they were destroyed on September 11, 2001), as a highly evocative testimony of lives and everyday practices that almost certainly left little or no trace in other historical records.

The focus of the book is on the various forms of needles, pins, thimbles, shears and scissors, and other related small implements, including their containers and some tools used in textile production such as lace and knitting, from the medieval period to the later nineteenth century. It covers material from Britain, Australia, Canada, and elsewhere, as well as the USA, its author's base. As a professor of archeology and anthropology at Boston University, Mary Beaudry draws on many seasons spent excavating the Spencer-Pierce-Little Farm (in Massachusetts) and her book is also rooted in work on the collections at the Winterthur Museum and Library. Its special contribution is to connect the production of these implements to their consumption/use in the practice of needle skills in the past, for domestic or commercial purposes. These small things are "read" here as a rich representation of larger aspects of social and cultural history, especially gendered identity. More specifically, Mary Beaudry wants to bring "multiple lines of evidence to bear on the interpretation of the material culture of sewing and needlework..."

REVIEWED BY BARBARA BURMAN

The author intends her book to be "a way for archaeologists to identify the material culture of needlework and sewing accurately and fully and to provide examples of contextual analysis ..." in support of her case that sewing and needle work took on "many meanings depending on when and where it was done, by whom it was done, and why it was done." As a fine example of this, she explores the use and meaning of thimbles excavated in Massachusetts at a site established by the seventeenth-century colonial missionary John Eliot in his work to convert indigenous Algonkian-speaking Indians to Christianity. Mary Beaudry argues for an interpretation of the thimbles (and sewing) as part of an attempted inculcation of European values and clothing. In her conclusion, she alerts archaeologists to the fact that near identical artifacts found at different sites—"domestic, institutional, religious, industrial"—can have different meanings and may have been used in different ways. She argues that it is therefore "critical" that the "specific historical and cultural context of individual sites" is delineated and case studies developed before interpretations aimed at elucidating wider cultural contexts are offered. This is presumably not news to her discipline. The caveat surely applies to the study of all kinds of widely used objects. For example, the chapter on straight pins shows how misleading it is to equate them solely with sewing and women. It is known they were used to fasten clothing of both sexes and headdresses, to fix paper documents together, and many other uses outside needlework. By using actual finds of pin fragments at a seventeenth-century burial site at Patuxent Point in Maryland and drawing on data from skeletal examinations, Mary Beaudry shows how pins were used in fastening winding sheets and shrouds, and how in this small community they were indicative of its wider economic and social practices.

The book has a uniform chapter structure: manufacturing and technological history of selected tool types and guidelines for dating them, followed by archeological case studies and suggestions to open up "possible avenues of interpretation." This occasionally frustrates discussion of general principles or wider historical possibilities inherent in the material and what might be implied by "context," but the value of the book lies in its orderly demonstration of specific methods and approaches. The book ends with a "wider consideration of the significance of sewing" as "a profession and as a pastime" and how excavated material culture of needlework and sewing can be used to illuminate lives of the past. Mary Beaudry cites *The Subversive Stitch* as providing "the framework" for *Findings* but prefers to not to overload her book with extensive historiography or with accounts of her own position within her discipline. She evidently subscribes to the "keep it short" approach. This makes for a refreshingly brief and tidy book. However, it also has the effect of underselling her own achievement. Her homage to Rosika Parker's *The Subversive Stitch* falls short of the fuller and timely engagement with it that her own work could offer.

Historical archeologists are not the only readers *Findings* will attract. The book is succinct and slim (and elegantly designed) but also suggestive, calling attention to the potential of interdisciplinarity. The author's search for ways to articulate interconnections between tools, techniques, and cultural practices will interest anyone looking for an example of "thinking with objects," cloth-related ones in particular. Its methodological consistency also provides useful comparative material for teaching and discussion. Admirers of the American historian Laurel Thatcher Ulrich will enjoy meeting up again with the spirited women involved in the disputed case of the missing bodkin, brought to court in Massachusetts in 1670 and cited in her *The Age of Homespun: Objects and Stories in the Creation of an American Myth*. It is reinterpreted in Mary Beaudry's section "A Tale of a Bodkin." The combination in *Findings* of manufacturing history and social and cultural history will also be attractive to museum curators engaged in documentation, interpretation, and display of these kinds of objects. It will interest makers and collectors who want to know more about what archeologists dig up and how it can deepen their understanding of the history and "cultural field" of the tools they handle or collect. There is still only a small body of literature concerned with the historical significance of needlework practices and *Findings* is a very welcome addition to it.

Broken Threads

The Destruction of the Jewish Fashion Industry in Germany and Austria

Edited by Roberta S. Kremer

Broken Threads tells the story of the destruction of the Jewish fashion industry under the Nazis.

Jewish designers were very prominent in the fashion industry of 1930s Germany and Austria. The emergence of Konfektion, or ready-to-wear, and the development of the modern department store, with its innovative merchandising and lavish interior design, only emphasized this prominence. The Nazis came to see German high fashion as too heavily influenced by Jewish designers, manufacturers and merchandisers. These groups were targeted with a campaign of propaganda, boycotts, humiliation and Aryanization.

Broken Threads chronicles this moment of cultural loss, detailing the rise of Jewish design and its destruction at the hands of the Nazis. Superbly illustrated with photographs and fashion plates from the collection of Claus Jahnke, *Broken Threads* explores this little-known part of fashion and of Nazi history.

2006 • 136pp • 82 bw illustrations • 270 x 180 mm
HB 978 1 84520 660 4 **£16.99** • **$29.95**

BERG

Order online at www.bergpublishers.com

The Textile Book

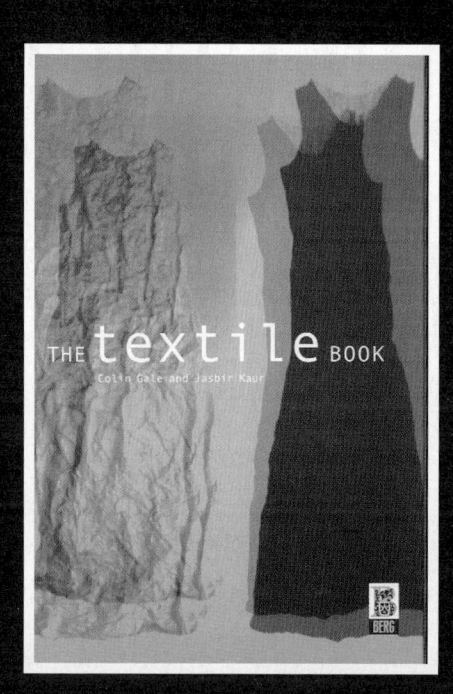

Colin Gale & Jasbir Kaur

Textiles are central to our lives and are at the heart of the world's largest industries. In recent years there has been a dynamic shift in attitudes toward textiles, fuelled in part by explosive developments in technology. While textiles have always retained roots in craft and industry, the discipline now embraces a much wider range of practices. Innovations in the industry demand a fresh approach to the subject, which this comprehensive introduction ably supplies.

Taking as their starting point the very meaning of textiles, Gale and Kaur go on to show the astonishing range of opportunities for careers in the field, from the creative (artists, craftspeople and designers) to the social and industrial, to the commercial and associated practices (buyers, journalists, researchers and scientists). *The Textile Book* takes us behind the scenes with professionals to reveal what various jobs involve, what influences decision makers, and how their decisions affect what we buy next season. What happens to clothes before they reach the shops? What determines the 'must have' item? How can recycled bottles be transformed into silk-like yarns? These and many other questions are explored to show the diversity that makes up the contemporary global textile scene.

2002 • 224pp • 8 colour and 30 bw illustrations
PB 978 1 85973 512 1 **£15.99 • $28.95**
HB 978 1 85973 507 7 **£50.00 • $99.95**

BERG

Order online at www.bergpublishers.com

CHANGING FASHION

A Critical Introduction to Trend Analysis and Cultural Meaning

From the Art Deco textile designs of Sonial Delaunay to the chameleonic shifts in Bob Dylan'ss appearance, this new book presents a fascinating range of contemporary and historical case material.

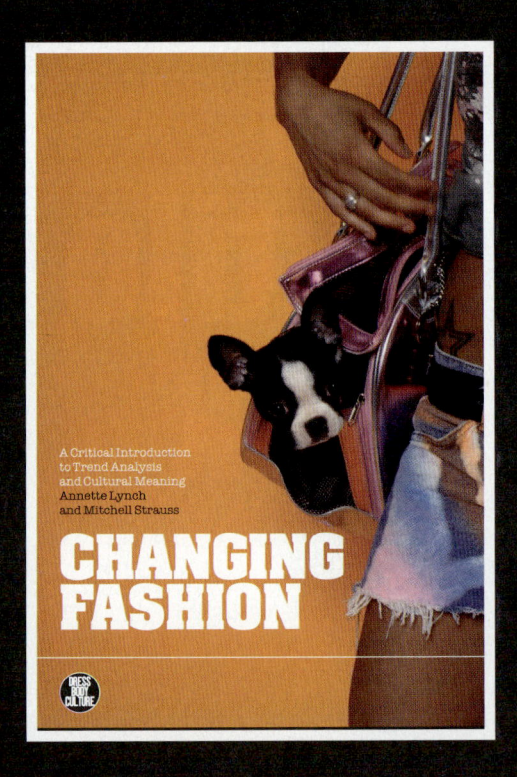

Annette Lynch and Mitchell Strauss

Changing trends in fashion have always reflected large-scale social and cultural changes. *Changing Fashion* presents for the first time a multi-disciplinary approach to examining fashion change, bringing together theory from fashion studies, cultural studies, sociology, psychology and art history, amongst others.

Ideal for the undergraduate student of fashion and cultural studies, the book has a wide range of contemporary and historical case material which provides practical examples of trend analysis and change. Key issues in fashion and identity, such as race, gender and consumption, are examined from different disciplinary angles to provide a critical overview of the field.

Changing Fashion provides a concise guide to the main theories across disciplines that explain how and why media, clothing styles, and cultural practices fall in and out of fashion.

August 2007 • 224pp • 192 x 156 mm
PB 978 1 84520 390 0 **£16.99** • **$29.95**
HB 978 1 84520 389 4 **£55.00** • **$99.95**

BERG

Order online at www.bergpublishers.com

a cultural history of fashion in the 20th century

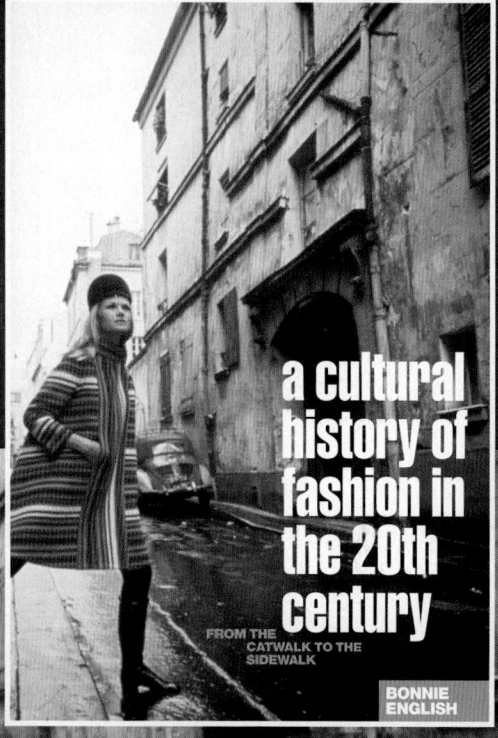

From the Catwalk to the Sidewalk

By Bonnie English

" Lively, accessible, highly informative, and drawing on an impressive range of both Eastern and Western examples, this is a unique contribution to fashion history. "
Becky E. Conekin, London College of Fashion

JULY 2007 • 224pp • 40bw illus
PB 978 1 84520 342 9 **£14.99** • **$24.95**
HB 978 1 84520 341 2 **£50.00** • **$94.95**

BERG

What caused the demise of haute couture in the twentieth century? What does the 'democratization' of fashion actually mean? Which key designers bridged the gap between 'couture', with its associations of elite class and taste, and 'street style', a product of tribalism and of popular culture and protest? If fashion imitates art and art imitates life, does life imitate fashion – do we wear the clothes or do the clothes wear us?

Setting fashion within its social, cultural and artistic context, *A Cultural History of Fashion in the 20th Century* presents an engaging history of the interplay between commerce and culture, technology and aesthetics, popular culture and pastiche, and fashion and anti-fashion.

Order online at www.bergpublishers.com

why women wear what they wear

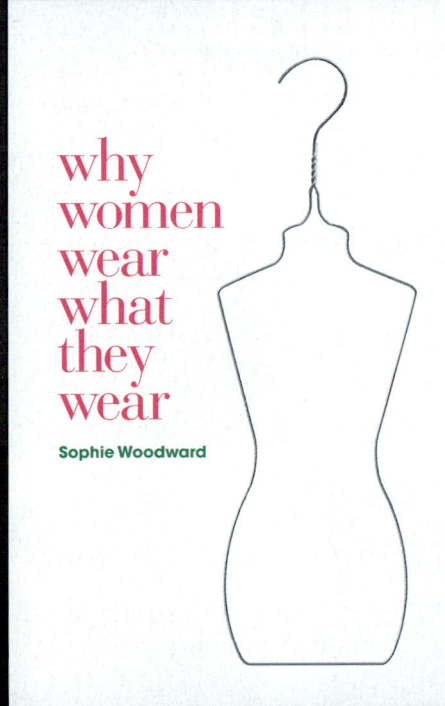

Sophie Woodward

Each morning we establish an image and an identity for ourselves through the simple act of getting dressed. *Why Women Wear What They Wear* presents an intimate ethnography of clothing choice.

The book uses real women's lives and clothing decisions – observed and discussed at the moment of getting dressed – to illustrate theories of clothing, the body and identity. Woodward pieces together what women actually think about clothing, dress and the body in a world where popular media and culture presents an increasingly extreme and distorted view of femininity and the ideal body.

Immediately accessible to all those who have stood in front of a mirror and wondered 'does this make me look fat?', 'is this skirt really me?' or 'does this jacket match?', *Why Women Wear What They Wear* provides students of anthropology and fashion with a fresh perspective on the social issues and constraints we are all consciously or unconsciously negotiating when we get dressed.

NOV 2007 • 224pp • 234 x 156 mm
PB 978 1 84520 699 4 **£19.99** • **$34.95**
HB 978 1 84520 698 7 **£55.00** • **$99.95**

BERG

Order online at www.bergpublishers.com

Old Clothes, New Looks

Second Hand Fashion

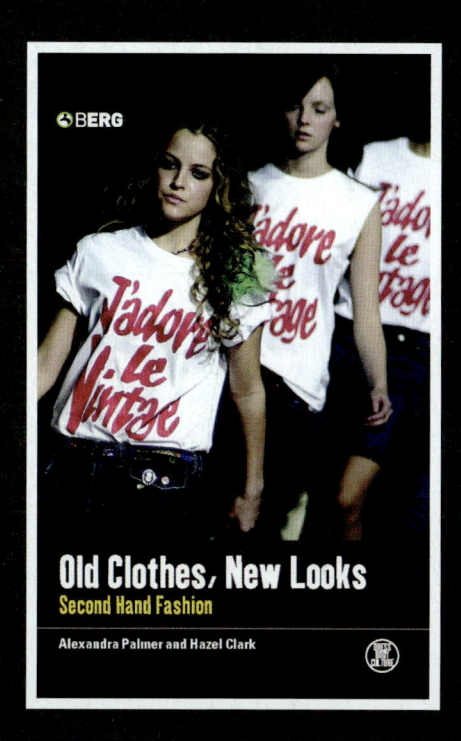

Edited by Alexandra Palmer and Hazel Clark

Recent interest in 'vintage' and second hand clothes by both fashion consumers and designers is only the latest manifestation of a long and complex cultural history of wearing and trading second hand clothes. With its origins in necessity, the passing of clothes between social and economic groups is now a global business, but with roots that are centuries old. To move from one social and cultural situation to another used clothes must be 'transformed' to become of potential value to a new social group. How, when and why this has happened is the subject of this book. *Old Clothes, New Looks* presents a three-part focus on the history, the trading culture, and the contemporary refashioning of second hand clothing. Historical perspectives include studies located in Renaissance Florence, early industrial England, colonial Australia, and mid twentieth-century Ireland. The global nature of the second hand trade in clothing is presented through original research from Zambia, India, the Philippines, Hong Kong, and Japan. The reuse of garments as contemporary fashion statements is explored through studies that include neo-mod retro-sixties subculture in Germany, the impact of 'vintage' in the USA on consumers and designers, as well as consideration of its sartorial and cultural challenges, encapsulated by the work of designer XULY.Bet. This groundbreaking book will be essential reading for all those interested in fashion and dress, material culture, consumption and anthropology, as well as to dealers, collectors and wearers of second hand clothes.

2004 • 272pp • 40 bw illustrations
PB 978 1 85973 857 3 **£16.99** • $28.95
HB 978 1 85973 852 8 **£55.00** • $99.95

BERG

Order online at www.bergpublishers.com

Textiles from India
The Global Trade

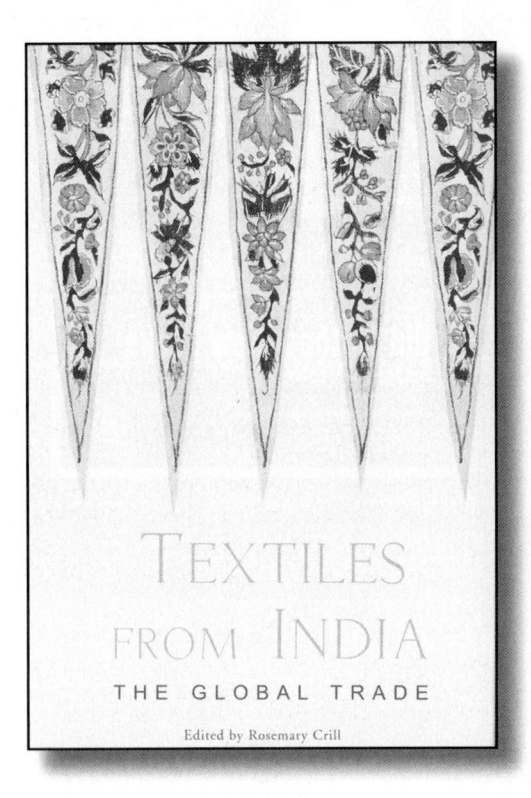

Edited by Rosemary Crill

For hundreds of years, textiles from India have travelled the globe, clothing the world, from kings and queens to the common man. Indian textiles have been traded in Europe, America, Africa, and the far east, often passing into ritual and religious custom. They have included the most exclusive and expensive festive fabrics as well as the common cloth used for daily wear.

Textiles from India explores this fascinating global history. Lavishly illustrated with over 250 colour photographs, the book covers the medieval period up to the present day. Among other case studies, we read about shawls from Kashmir making their way across Asia; brocades especially woven in Benaras for Buddhist rituals in Tibet; the muslins of Bengal; and the perennial European favourites of block prints and chintz.

430pp • 260 colour illus
ISBN 978 1 90542 217 3 (HB) £39.99 • $75.00

Order online at www.bergpublishers.com

Seagull BOOKS

Notes for Contributors

Articles should be approximately 25 pages in length and must include a three-sentence biography of the author(s) and an abstract. Interviews should not exceed 15 pages and do not require an author biography. Exhibition and book reviews are normally 500 to 2,000 words in length. The Publishers will require a disk as well as a hard copy of any contributions (please mark clearly on the disk what word-processing program has been used). Berg accepts most programs with the exception of Clarisworks.

Textile: The Journal of Cloth & Culture will produce one issue a year devoted to a single topic. Persons wishing to organize a topical issue are invited to submit a proposal which contains a hundred-word description of the topic together with a list of potential contributors and paper subjects. Proposals are accepted only after review by the journal editors and in-house editorial staff at Berg.

Manuscripts
Manuscripts should be submitted to one of the editors. Further submission details can be obtained by emailing Janet Gilburt (rooster.gilburt@virgin.net). Manuscripts will be acknowledged by the editor and entered into the review process discussed below. Manuscripts without illustrations will not be returned unless the author provides a self-addressed stamped envelope. Submission of a manuscript to the journal will be taken to imply that it is not being considered elsewhere for publication, and that if accepted for publication, it will not be published elsewhere, in the same form, in any language, without the consent of the editor and publisher. It is a condition of acceptance by the editor of a manuscript for publication that the publishers automatically acquire the copyright of the published article throughout the world. *Textile: The Journal of Cloth & Culture* does not pay authors for their manuscripts nor does it provide retyping, drawing, or mounting of illustrations.

Style
U.S. spelling and mechanicals are to be used. Authors are advised to consult *The Chicago Manual of Style (15th Edition)* as a guideline for style. Webster's Dictionary is our arbiter of spelling. We encourage the use of major subheadings and, where appropriate, second-level subheadings. Manuscripts submitted for consideration as an article must contain: a title page with the full title of the article, the author(s) name and address, a three-sentence biography for each author, and a 200 word abstract. Do not place the author's name on any other page of the manuscript.

Manuscript Preparation
Manuscripts must be typed double-spaced (including quotations, notes, and references cited), one side only, with at least one-inch margins on standard paper using a typeface no smaller than 12pts. The original manuscript and a copy of the text on disk *(please ensure it is clearly marked with the word-processing program that has been used) must* be submitted, along with color *original* photographs (to be returned). Authors should retain a copy for their records. Any necessary artwork must be submitted with the manuscript.

Footnotes
Footnotes appear as "Notes" at the end of articles. Authors are advised to include footnote material in the text whenever possible. Notes are to be numbered consecutively throughout the paper and are to be typed double-spaced at the end of the text. (Do not use any footnoting or end-noting programs that your software may offer as this text becomes irretrievably lost at the typesetting stage.)

References
The list of references should be limited to, and inclusive of, those publications actually cited in the text. References are to be cited in the body of the text in parentheses with the author's last name, the year of original publication, and page number—e.g. (Rouch 1958: 45). Titles and publication information appear as "References" at the end of the article and should be listed alphabetically by author and chronologically for each author. Names of journals and publications should appear in full. Film and video information appears as "Filmography". References cited should be typed double-spaced on a separate page. *References not presented in the style required will be returned to the author for revision.*

Tables
All tabular material should be part of a separately numbered series of "Tables." Each table must be typed on a separate sheet and identified by a short descriptive title. Footnotes for tables appear at the bottom of the table. Marginal notations on manuscripts should indicate approximately where tables are to appear.

Figures
All illustrative material (drawings, maps, diagrams, and photographs) should be designated "Figures." They must be submitted in a form suitable for publication without redrawing. Drawings should be carefully done with black ink on either hard, white, smooth-surfaced board or good quality tracing paper. Ordinarily, computer-generated drawings are not of publishable quality. Color photographs are encouraged by the publishers. Whenever possible, photographs should be 8 × 10 inches. The publishers encourage artwork to be submitted as scanned files (600 dpi or above) on disk or via email. All figures should be clearly numbered on the back and numbered consecutively. All captions should be typed double-spaced on a separate page. Marginal notations on manuscripts should indicate approximately where figures are to appear. While the editors and publishers will use ordinary care in protecting all figures submitted, they cannot assume responsibility for their loss or damage. Authors are discouraged from submitting rare or non-replaceable materials. It is the author's responsibility to secure written copyright clearance on all photographs and drawings that are not in the public domain. Copyright should be obtained for worldwide rights and on-line publishing.

Criteria for Evaluation
Textile: The Journal of Cloth & Culture is a refereed journal. Manuscripts will be accepted only after review by both the editors and anonymous reviewers deemed competent to make professional judgments concerning the quality of the manuscript. Upon request, authors will receive reviewers' evaluations.